MEN, MOTORS, AND MARKETS
by Dean Russell

by Dean Russell

The TVA Idea

Men, Motors, and Markets

Translator of Frederic Bastiat's *The Law*

SPECIAL EDITION — Privately printed for the Atwood Vacuum Machine Company
Copyright 1959 by Dean Russell
All rights reserved
Printed in U. S. A.

Contents

Chapters	Page
Dedication	1
1. How to Disemploy a Slave	3
2. They Raced Them Around the World	21
3. If War Should Come	41
4. From the Cradle to the Grave	55
5. Meanwhile, Back on the Farm	71
6. How to Stay Alive on the Roads	85
7. The Last Billionaire	101
8. How to Get to the Top	113
9. How Much Is an Executive Worth?	127
10. Where Men Are Free to Try	139
11. The Silent Partner	153
Bibliography	165
Index	167

50 years of service as an
internal auto body
hardware supplier

- 5 plants totaling 10 acres under roof
- 1800 employees
- Door hinges, door latches, hood hinges, hood latches, trunk hinges, trunk locks, seat adjusters, props, window regulators, parking brake mechanisms and contract assemblies.

Dedication

There are around 4,300,000 privately owned businesses in the United States, and more than four million of them are classified as "small businesses." Every day, almost 1,000 new companies join the parade — and about 500 drop out.

Among these typical small businesses that generate the primary strength of a free America are the companies that produce parts for the large automobile manufacturers. There are many thousands of them — if you include firms like the hunting and trapping company in Alaska that supplies the tough walrus hides that are used for friction drives in coil winding machines. More than 80 per cent of the total automobile parts business, however, is done by around 400 companies.

About 50 per cent of every General Motors car is composed of parts made by independent suppliers. For Ford, the figure is 59 per cent — and for Chrysler, 65 per cent. The parts supplied by these outside producers range from complete frames and radiators to seat covers and light bulbs.

Currently, these independent producers sell about $3 billion worth of original equipment each year to the automobile companies — plus $2 billion worth of tires, batteries, and other replacement parts directly to the public. They employ more than 400,000 persons.

During the early history of the automobile industry, practically *every* part of the car was produced by the independent manufacturers of parts. The automobile companies merely assembled the parts into a complete car. And as often as not, it was the parts manufacturers, instead of the automobile companies, who were responsible for dramatic improvements to the car — curtains, windshields and wipers, electric ignition, lighting, self-starters, and so on. And still today, the automobile companies depend to a large extent on the engineering genius of the parts makers for new ideas on how to improve the manufacturing processes and quality of parts for each successive model.

Among the pioneer producers of automobile parts was the Atwood Vacuum Machine Company of Rockford, Illinois. It was founded in 1909 by two brothers, J. T. and S. B. Atwood — and Mr. Seth B. Atwood is still active as Chairman of the Board. This Special Edition of "Men, Motors, and Markets" is issued in commemoration of the Fiftieth Anniversary of that event.

Chapter 1
HOW TO DISEMPLOY A SLAVE

The year 1787 covered two events that were to have a profound effect on the American people and the way we live. First, and by far the most important, the founders of this nation met in Philadelphia to draft a constitution for a new idea in government. Second, the free state of Maryland granted to Oliver Evans a patent on his drawings for a new idea in transportation — "a Steam-Carriage . . . to move . . . without the aid of animal force" on the roads of that state.

In September of 1787, the work of that Constitutional Convention was finished and submitted to the people of the 13 independent states for their approval. Some 18 months later, the new government came into formal existence. And on December 14, 1792, Evans petitioned it to grant him a *national* patent to replace his several state patents for a "land carriage without cattle."

It took Oliver Evans another 13 years to actually construct his self-propelled road vehicle. Like the Constitution, its birthplace was also Philadelphia. On or near the tenth day of July, 1805, his steam vehicle, the *Orukter Amphibolos*, moved ponderously up Market Street under its own power to Center Square. America's first "automobile" was on the road — and no newspaper bothered to record either the date or the event itself! For several days thereafter, Evans entertained the good people of the City of Brotherly Love by driving his vehicle around the square. Then, since his machine was built to operate on both land and water, he astounded them by driving it into the Schuylkill River. (That same idea was used with great success some 137 years later by our armed forces in World War Two.) In 1813, Evans predicted that "The time will come when the people will travel [in road carriages] . . . almost as fast as birds can fly."

This book is dedicated primarily to the second of the above early landmarks in American history — the birth and growth of the automobile and its impact on the way we live. But the fundamental ideas contained in the first one — that is, a free people operating under a representative form of government in a competitive economy — will necessarily play a vital part in the story.

While Oliver Evans built the first *American* road vehicle that ran under its own power, he was by no means the "father" of the automobile. A French artillery captain, Nicholas Cugnot, was ahead of him by 36 years. In 1769, he used a steam engine as the source of power for a self-propelled gun carriage. That clumsy, three-wheeled, barely workable vehicle has an excellent claim to first place in the direct ancestry of the magnificent automobile you drive today.

The first passenger automobile – invented by Richard Trevithick — began operating on the roads of England in 1801. The patented plans of Oliver Evans' proposed steam-powered vehicle were readily available in England during the 1790's, and it is generally presumed that Trevithick was familiar with them. In turn, it is certain that the published details and drawings of Trevithick's successful road carriage had been studied by Evans before he completed his own amphibious model in 1805. And both of them, of course, were familiar with the stationary steam engine that had been invented long before their time.

Actually, Hero of Alexandria may have started the whole thing about 130 years before the birth of Christ when he invented a sort of toy that was run by steam. But for the next 1800 years, that magnificent source of power lay largely dormant. While several men in various countries experimented with steam power in the 1600's, it wasn't until 1705 that Thomas Newcomen developed the first workable steam engine. It was used to pump water from British coal mines. That engine, however, was too primitive for general use. It remained for James Watt, beginning in 1762 and continuing through 1782, to

Photo Courtesy A.M.A.

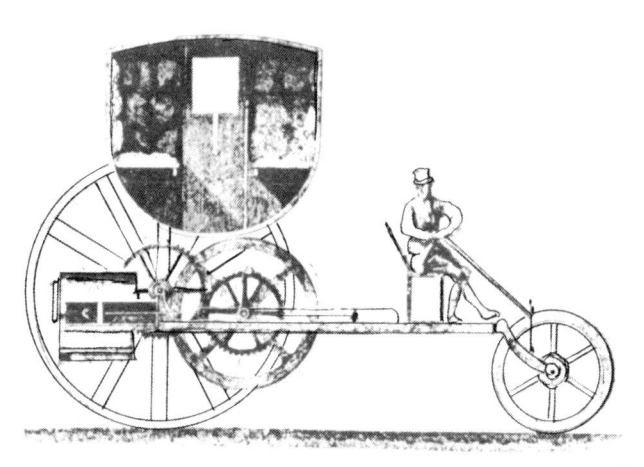

ANCESTOR OF THE AUTOMOBILE
Reconstruction of Cugnot's 1769
Artillery Carriage

Photo Courtesy Duncan, H. O.
"The World on Wheels"

Trevithick's First Carriage
(From 1801 Patent Application)

Artist's Conception of Orukter Amphibolos
Philadelphia, 1805

Ten Miles Per Hour; England, 1810

Sir Goldsworthy Gurney's Passenger Bus
London to Bath, 1829

Photos Courtesy G-M

perfect a practical and versatile steam engine that could be used as the source of power for factories, ships, trains, and automobiles. That event ushered in the modern machine age. And as we shall shortly see, the increasing growth of steam-powered factories and transportation facilities was soon to have a most dramatic impact on the way people lived and thought — including their attitude toward the age-old institution of human slavery. While the automobile itself played only a small and indirect part in the abolition of slavery, it is still a recordable fact that it, too, helped to destroy that most ancient curse of mankind.

Well before 1800, Watt's steam engine was being used extensively by various English manufacturers — in flour mills, breweries, textile factories, and so on. William Murdock, the inventor of gas lighting, also used that source of power for a crude train that ran on oak rails in British quarries and coal pits in 1784. And in 1815, another Englishman, George Stephenson, converted Murdock's primitive seven-mile-an-hour locomotive into the early Nineteenth Century model that was soon doing 70 miles an hour on metal rails. The steam (and sail) ship "Savannah" crossed the Atlantic from Georgia to Liverpool in 1819. In Springfield, Massachusetts, in 1825, Thomas Blanchard produced the first *practical* steam road carriage in America. In addition to easy steering, it contained the then-novel feature of a workable reverse gear.

Throughout this period, those "steamers" were becoming increasingly popular in England. Sir Goldsworthy Gurney built a succession of them after 1820. The model he built in 1829 made a sustained journey from London to Bath and return, a distance of 200 miles at a speed of 15 miles per hour. During the early 1830's, more than a hundred steam automobiles of various designs were operating on the roads of England. Six of them were large passenger buses, built by Walter Hancock. In a period of three months, one of his buses traveled 4,200 miles and carried 12,761 passengers, without an accident or serious delay. By the mid-1830's, steam engines were the source of cheap power for an extensive industrial complex (manufacturing and transportation) in Western Europe and the United States. For better or for worse, the modern age of mass-produced and low-cost industrial products was in full swing.

Karl Marx (and others) reached the conclusion that it was unquestionably for the worse. And, admittedly, they produced some telling evidence and persuasive ideas to support their convictions. But perhaps they were so busy slashing at the individual trees that they had no idea at all of the vast forest with which they were dealing. They condemned the age of mechanical power because it brought women and children into the deplorable factories of that era — at meager wages and long hours of killing labor. But the picture they drew was far from complete because, among other things, they utterly ignored the part that the mechanical revolution in transportation and production was playing in the abolition of the most ancient curse of mankind — legalized human slavery.

We know that the institution of slavery is as old as the recorded history of man. For example, it appears in the laws of Hammurabi. We know, further, that it continued to exist throughout most of the world until well into the Nineteenth Century. There is, however, no general agreement as to the principal cause of its abolition.

It is certainly safe to say that government itself wasn't responsible for abolishing human bondage. If a government wants to stay in business, its actions must generally reflect the attitudes and desires of the people under its authority. So the actual laws that were written against slavery were primarily acknowledgements of an existing situation that had developed from other causes.

Nor was education, as such, responsible for ending slavery; the educated classes throughout the ages had generally tolerated, justified, and supported the institution. If they hadn't, it couldn't possibly have continued to exist. And to say that the people in general were responsible for abolishing human bondage, still leaves unanswered their reasons for doing so. Was the answer Christianity? To some considerable extent, yes. But if that were the primary answer, one would still be faced with the awkward task of explaining why we Christians required some 1900 years to complete the job. The Columbia Encyclopedia (and other standard references) acknowledges the great part played by Christianity, and then goes on to the part played by machinery and the capitalist economy:

"The introduction of Christianity is generally thought to have had little effect [on slavery during the first few hundred years of the Christian Era], though it did mitigate conditions by inculcating principles of humanity, and it did give hope and courage to the long-oppressed classes. . . . In Western Europe, outright slavery had largely disappeared by the later Middle Ages, though it still remained in such manifestations as the use of slaves on galleys. . . . The British, the Dutch, the French, the Spanish, and the Portugese all engaged in the [African] slave traffic [beginning in the Sixteenth Century and continuing well into the Nineteenth]. . . . The British, in abolishing slavery, were primarily motivated by economic, not humanitarian, interests. While the institution produced great wealth under the mercantilist system, it became unprofitable with the rise of industrial capitalism."

That industrial capitalism included steam ships, steam trains, and steam automobiles — as well as steam-driven machines in factories.

H. G. Wells, in his "The Outline of History," discusses the same idea:

"A vast proportion of mankind in the early civilizations was employed in purely mechanical drudgery. At its onset, power-driven machinery did not seem to promise any release from such unintelligent toil. . . . [But as the mechanical revolution] went on, the plain logic of the new situation asserted itself more clearly. Human beings were no longer wanted as a source of mere indiscriminated power. What could be done mechanically by a human being could be done faster and better by a machine."

Whatever else slaves might be used for, it is dead certain that they could never be trusted with the responsibility of operating the power-driven ships, trains, automobiles, and factory machines that were becoming increasingly common in the western world of the late Eighteenth and early Nineteenth Centuries. Thus the ever-present moral arguments against slavery were soon buttressed by the overriding economic arguments against it.

Beginning in 1833, Parliament rapidly outlawed the practice of slavery throughout the vast British Empire. (In the home islands themselves, a 1772 court decision had already decreed that the 15,000 or so imported slaves in Britain at that time were automatically free men because "as soon as a slave set his foot on the soil of the British islands he became free.") Slavery in the French Empire was abolished in 1848. Russia liberated her slaves in 1861. Slavery in the Dutch Empire was outlawed in 1863. Brazil continued the practice until 1888. Even today, slavery continues to exist in various nations and areas where the primary source of transportation and power has long been the muscles of men and animals. *

Of course, it could have been merely a remarkable coincidence that slavery diminished as mechanical sources of power and transportation increased, but that hardly seems likely. Suppose, for example, that the automobile industry could produce 170 million cars in a slave society; what in the world would it do with them! But what about slavery in the United States? Since this nation had as many or more machines than the others, why wasn't slavery voluntarily abolished here? The history of human bondage in the United States also lends support (with a reverse twist) to the theory that machines, rather than morality or education, may have been of primary importance in determining the issue of slavery. Roger Burlingame, in his "Backgrounds of Power," explains that reverse twist while dis-

---

*Information on present-day slavery may be secured from the "United Nations Committee on Slavery."

cussing Eli Whitney's 1793 invention of the gin for cleaning cotton:

> "The gin led directly to a social, economic, and political crisis. By increasing a hundredfold the productivity per worker in separating short-staple cotton from its tenacious seeds, it produced an unbalance between cleaning and picking, planting and cultivation. The faster the cotton was cleaned, the more labor was required in the field. Thus slavery, moribund in 1790, became a dominant institution. . . ."

The idea of human slavery was completely foreign to the precepts on which this nation was founded. And when the Constitution of the United States was drafted, the founders wrote into it the first necessary steps toward its abolition. Thus it is probable that this country would have led all others in abolishing human slavery, if Whitney had invented a cotton picker along with his cotton cleaner.

Before the cotton gin, not much cotton was grown in the South because it was too expensive to clean by hand — even when the hands belonged to a slave. But Whitney's first crude machine enabled a man to clean 50 pounds of cotton a day, and rapid improvements to the machine soon doubled that amount. The resulting demand for cotton caused its cultivation to become highly profitable. But picking cotton was such a backbreaking and monotonous task that it was the last job a free man would take. Since there was no machine to relieve the drudgery of the job — and since no education or skill was required — it automatically fell to slaves.

Before Whitney's invention, slavery was rapidly becoming both unprofitable and immoral — in Alabama as well as in Massachusetts. But with the gin, slave labor became highly profitable in the hot areas of the country where cotton could be grown. In due course, most educators, legislators, and churchmen in the South were soon defending or tolerating the "peculiar institution" — or were remaining discreetly silent about it.

A modern cotton picking machine would have been of vast help in abolishing slavery by again making it uneconomic, and thus permitting the long-suppressed moral ideas against it to take effect. But, most unfortunately, such a machine was not invented for more than a hundred years after the gin. Thus the issue of slavery in the United States was settled by a fratricidal war. The side with the best factories and transportation won, and the slaves were set free. That was as it should have been. But it is to be hoped that a few of the victors stopped to ponder the probability that it was more a matter of climate and economics, rather than morality and government, that determined which side was which.

As we have noted, the labor-saving machines that helped to disemploy the slaves of the Nineteenth Century were generally based on the steam engine of Newcomen and Watt. In that early period of steam-powered vehicles, England was unquestionably the leader. It held that leadership for many years in the development of locomotives, ships, and stationary steam engines for factory uses. But England lost out in the development of road vehicles because of restrictive legislation. Beginning in 1835, legal restrictions against automobiles on English roads became increasingly severe. It was claimed that those heavy steam cars were scaring horses and ruining the road surfaces. Finally, in 1865, Parliament decreed that no self-propelled vehicle could operate on English roads unless it was preceded by a man *on foot* carrying a red flag. The law wasn't repealed until 1896.

But in spite of those restrictions, various inventors continued their efforts to find a better source of power than steam for their automobiles. For example, Robert Anderson, a Scotsman, used a primitive electric motor as the source of power for a road carriage in Aberdeen in 1839. Toward the end of the century, vehicles that drew their power from electric batteries were to become exceedingly popular in both Europe and the United

States. They served as the first taxicabs before 1890.

If just one person had to be selected as the "father" of the gasoline automobile, that person would unquestionably be Jean Joseph Etienne Lenoir of Luxembourg. In 1860, while living in Paris, he secured a patent on the world's first useable internal combustion engine. Like its impractical predecessors, it was a two-stroke mechanism that employed an electric spark to ignite a mixture of illuminating gas and air. The main difference was that Lenoir's engine worked. In fact, it was so successful that he attempted to install it in a road carriage. But he soon decided that liquid petroleum would be a better fuel for an automobile than was illuminating gas. So he built another engine for that purpose. At an unspecified date in 1863, he installed his new engine in the carriage he had already built, and drove it from his Paris carriage factory to Joinville-le-Point and back. He covered the 15 miles in three hours, including stops. For several years thereafter, he continued to drive his automobile around Paris. But he seemed to regard it merely as a personal hobby while he devoted his full efforts to producing his highly successful stationary engines.

Three young Germans — Nikolaus Otto, Gottlieb Daimler, and Karl Benz — were greatly influenced by the work of Lenoir, whom they knew personally. Beginning in 1860, they were all soon working on new engines. In 1877, Otto secured a patent on his four-cycle engine, and is thus generally credited with an invention that Siegfried Marcus of Vienna had made four or five years earlier — and that a Frenchman, Beau de Rochas, had worked out in theory in 1862. During the year 1885, both Daimler and Benz installed engines of their own designs in crude road vehicles and ran them successfully. Those two names soon became famous in the expanding automobile industries of Germany and France in the early 1890's.

In the United States, George Brayton applied for a patent on a gasoline engine in 1872. While his engine was used experimentally to power a trolley car, it was never successful in a road vehicle. That was the engine, however, that inspired George Selden to apply for the first American patent on a road vehicle to be powered by an internal combustion engine using gasoline. While the application was filed in 1879, it wasn't finally issued until 1895. Selden himself contributed absolutely nothing to the development of the automobile.

The Duryea brothers (Frank and Charles), have generally received credit for inventing and building the first gasoline automobile in America. It was publicly road-tested on September 20, 1893. But as frequently happens in this area of "firsts," there is considerable evidence to indicate that several others may have been ahead of them with "experimental models." It's not important — for the fact remains that the Duryea car was the first practical or successful American gasoline automobile. The magazine, *Horseless Age,* later estimated that during the early 1890's, perhaps as many as three hundred other American tinkerers and mechanics had been experimenting with their own particular ideas as to how to build a "horseless carriage"!

In 1900, the first automobile show was held in Madison Square Garden, New York City. Thirty-one different cars were exhibited, of which not one is being manufactured today. That same year, the first automobile advertisement appeared in *The Saturday Evening Post*. The automobile age had arrived.

The above chronology of the early development of the automobile is, of course, absurdly sketchy. It completely ignores the story of how both air and water were used to cool the engine. It doesn't even mention the fact that a hard-rubber tire was first used in 1845 — nor the fact that without the modern air-filled tire invented in 1889 by the Scotsman, John B. Dunlop, there couldn't possibly have been an automobile industry as we now know it. No credit is here given to the many thousands of inventors who made improvements upon the work of their predecessors. The story of improved steering mechanisms and differential devices to permit vehicles to turn corners is skipped entirely. And so on and so on.

Photo Courtesy L'Automobile, Paris

FIRST GASOLINE AUTOMOBILE
Reconstruction of Lenoir's 1863 car

THE ELECTRIC "HANSOM" WAS POPULAR IN THE 1890's

Photo Courtesy A.M.A.

15

FIRST AMERICAN GASOLINE CAR
Duryea Brothers' 1893 "Horseless Carriage"

Photos Courtesy A.M.A.

The Stanley Twins in Their First "Steamer," 1896

There are two reasons for here offering such a brief history of the ancestry of your modern automobile. First, we would have to know who invented the wheel before we could allocate credit to the inventors of the automobile. Actually, the automobile was invented by many thousands of persons. It is still being invented today by any person who thinks of a way to improve it. (One out of every six current patent applications is still "automotive.") In the year 2000, our grandchildren will doubtless wonder how we ever managed to get around in those old contraptions of the 1950's. So the above chronology attempts merely to hit the high spots. And even then, there is no sure way of knowing that the right persons were picked for that. For example, the first vehicle that looked even remotely like an automobile as we know it today was constructed in 1892 by the Frenchman, Emile Levassor, who merely combined the various inventions of others into an integrated whole.

The second reason for such short treatment of the ancestors of the automobile is that this study is not offered as a history. The primary objective of this book is to ask *why* certain things happened in this area, and to speculate as to what those events have meant to mankind in general. For example, we have already briefly examined the part played by mechanical power and transportation in the abolition of human slavery. Another (and far less important) event in the story of the automobile was the battle for supremacy among steam, electricity, and gasoline as the source of power. Why was gasoline the winner? What effect, if any, did that decision have on our economy and life in general?

Each of those three sources of power had its advantages and disadvantages. Steam gave smooth acceleration, and the driver didn't have to worry about shifting gears or stalling on a hill. Perhaps its greatest advantage lay in the fact that it was the logical and best known source of power during the early stages of the development of the automobile. But even the best of the steam vehicles still had to be "fired up" before they would run, and the drivers of the early models needed considerable engineering skill. For a long trip, there was no convenient way to carry the heavy load of necessary fuel. Even so, for many years after 1896 and the appearance of the Stanley Steamer (and the White Steamer and others), thousands of inventors, investors, and customers continued to bet their time and money on the future of the steam-powered automobile. Those "steamers" were still manufactured and entered in the annual Automobile Show as late as 1923. Even today, when they appear in the various shows and parades of old automobiles, they attract far more attention than do the old electrics.

But electric power was quiet, clean, and safe. And the mechanical requirements for that source of power were the simplest of the three. Unfortunately, the fuel load (battery) was extremely heavy, the radius of operation was short, and the necessity of recharging the battery was even more annoying than getting up steam in a boiler-powered car. Even so, the fact that *women* could easily start and safely drive the electric cars delayed for several years the final decision for gasoline as the best source of power.

Unfortunately for the backers of gasoline power, their early engines were noisy and complicated to operate. Also, they seemed always to be breaking down. In both fact and song, the driver frequently had to "get out and get under." But gasoline meant a quick-starting vehicle with great power in comparison to its weight. The early gasoline cars were far more adaptable to the horrible road conditions of that time. It was comparatively easy to carry sufficient fuel for a reasonably long trip. Better still, gasoline was widely available even at that early stage. And the discovery of vast reserves of oil in Texas in 1901 insured a plentiful and cheap supply of that handy fuel. But probably most important of all, the purchase price of the gasoline-powered cars was generally lower than that for steam or electricity.

Whatever their reasons, at the turn of the century the people began buying more gasoline cars than steam or electric ones. In a free economy, that fact always determines the winner. Thus the automobile is almost solely responsible for bringing into existence the oil industry as we know it today — and for sending our geologists, engineers, and businessmen scurrying all over the world in a continuing campaign to find and develop even more sources of that vital fuel.

This brings us to the beginning of the Twentieth Century and what has been aptly called "the age of the automobile." By then, human slavery had long since disappeared from the United States. But human drudgery was still with us. As we shall see, the automotive industry was destined to play a large part in reducing that drudgery while increasing the earning capacity of the people in general — and thus contributing materially to a higher level of living for all.

Chapter 2
THEY RACED THEM AROUND THE WORLD

In 1908, a "race around the world" for stock cars was sponsored by *The New York Times*. The race was from New York City to Paris — by way of Alaska and Siberia — and was open to all comers. There were scores of applicants from several countries, including four Americans. But when the race finally started from Times Square on February 12, there were five foreign entries and only one American — a Thomas "Flyer" driven by Montague Roberts, and with George Schuster riding as mechanic. Some 200,000 New Yorkers cheered the contestants on their way. Newspaper coverage and popular interest remained high throughout the race.

Only two of the six cars made it across the United States — the American entry and a German "Protos" — with the Flyer ahead by about a month. In San Francisco, the mechanic Schuster became the driver, and the car was shipped to Alaska for the second leg of the around-the-world race. At that point, however, the judges decided not to go through Alaska as planned but to ship the two cars direct to the Siberian seaport of Vladivostok and to continue from there. Because the American entry was so far ahead when the change was made, Schuster was awarded a 30-day "credit" over his rival when they resumed the race toward Paris from Vladivostok — by way of Manchuria, Russia, and Germany.

Schuster rolled into Paris four days behind his German rival. But because of the 30-day credit the Flyer had piled up in the United States and Alaska, the American entry was declared the winner by 26 days. Schuster arrived in Paris 170 days after leaving New York. One admirer of the fantasies of Jules Verne added 10 days for shipping the Flyer across the Atlantic and reported the story under the title, "Around the World in 180

21

Days." Schuster was actually on the road (or, at any rate, driving on land) for 88 days and a total distance of 13,431 miles. That victory (and the resulting publicity) rescued the Thomas Motor Car Company from a shaky financial position and turned it into a highly profitable enterprise.

Before 1908 and that "around the world" feat, American cars were generally considered inferior to the European makes — by American purchasers as well as others. But after winning that test for ruggedness (plus another award the same year for excellence of manufacture), American cars soon became popular all over the world. That second award, for "standardization and interchangeability of parts," was made to Cadillac by the Royal Automobile Club of London. Three Cadillacs had been selected at random from stock in the United States and shipped to the officials of the Club in England. Under their supervision, the cars were completely disassembled and the parts were piled indiscriminately together. Cadillac mechanics then assembled three cars from the thoroughly mixed parts. The cars were put through various road tests, with all three Cadillacs making perfect scores. That "Sir Thomas Dewar trophy" was won again by Cadillac in 1913 for its electrical starting, lighting, and ignition — the only automobile ever to win the trophy twice.

The Cadillac is still with us. But the Flyer is now merely another of the more than 2700 brand names that have long since ceased to exist. For advertising purposes, however, today's automobiles are still climbing mountains and crossing deserts all over the world. Apparently, speed and performance records still have a powerful appeal for potential purchasers. That tried and true type of advertising probably started way back in 1865 with Sylvester Hayward Roper and his "improved steam carriage." To show the excellence of his road carriages, he pitted one of them against a racing horse and a running man in a mile race at Poughkeepsie, New York. The man covered the mile in 5 minutes and 20 seconds. The horse did it in 2 minutes and 37 seconds. But the steam carriage won the contest with a

The Thomas "Flyer" around the world

Alexander Winton
and His Dos-A-Dos

Photos Courtesy A.M.A.

Indianapolis Speedway, 1909

1903—Barney Oldfield at Tiller of Ford's "999"

Mrs. Joan Newton Cuneo

Photos Courtesy A.M.A.

24

time of 2 minutes and 20 seconds.

The first real automobile race in the United States was sponsored by the *Chicago Times-Herald* on Thanksgiving Day, 1895 — from Chicago to Evanston and return. The total prize money at stake was $5,000. Six cars started the 52 mile race. A "Duryea" gasoline car, driven by Frank Duryea himself, was the winner. He averaged a little less than seven miles per hour over fearfully bad roads in snow and mud. But even then, he still defeated an imported Benz that had been a prize winner in the Paris-Bordeaux race earlier in the year. The $2,000 first prize money was of great help to the newly established Duryea Motor Wagon Company in Springfield, Massachusetts. In 1896, that company produced 13 gasoline motorcars.

In 1897, Alexander Winton raced one mile in one minute and 48 seconds in a car of his own design. Later in the year, he drove the car 800 miles from Cleveland to New York in 10 days. Those two feats made the Winton a strong rival of the Duryea. When a 10 mile race sponsored by the *Chicago Inter-Ocean* in September of 1900 was won by Winton in 16 minutes and two seconds, his cars became the most popular in the nation.

By the end of 1900, there were something like 100 manufacturers of automobiles in the United States. Among those manufacturers were Ford, Olds, Winton, the Duryea brothers, F. E. and F. O. Stanley, James Packard, the General Electric Company, and those six Mack brothers who built their first experimental "bus-truck" in Brooklyn, New York in 1900. Total production for the year was 4,192 vehicles — steam, electric, and gasoline.

In 1901, young Roy Chapin drove a one-cylinder Oldsmobile from Detroit, across Canada, down the towpaths of the Erie Canal, and on to the Automobile Show in New York City. That seven-and-one-half-day trip caught the public fancy — and Oldsmobile sales shot up from 425 in 1901 to 2,500 in 1902. The following year, an Olds racing car at Daytona Beach covered five miles in six and one-half minutes — and sales continued upward. That was also the year that three cars were driven across the continent from San Francisco to New York — a Winton, a Packard, and an Oldsmobile. (The Winton, driven by Dr. H. N. Jackson, did it first, May 23 to July 26.) In 1904, the Olds Motor Works sold 5,000 of its "curved-dash runabouts" at $650 each "with mudguards." That was more than 20 per cent of all the automobiles produced in the United States during the year. The next year, Gus Edwards wrote "In My Merry Oldsmobile," and total production of both the curved-dash and straight-dash models was 11,500 cars. Unquestionably, the Oldsmobile was the first mass-produced and low-priced automobile in the world. Even so, the manufacturers of the more than one million horse drawn vehicles in 1905 continued to expand their facilities.

The girl and the automobile were early the subject of popular songs and plays. The song "Love In An Automobile" appeared in 1899. It was soon followed by "The Automobile Honeymoon." Other song writers tried their luck with titles like "Take Me Out In A Velie Car" and "Give Me A Spin In Your Mitchell, Bill." The stage first saw the automobile in 1904 in "The Great Automobile Mystery." In his report on the play, one critic punned, "The tragedy scenes are breathed hard a la Panhard."

In 1903, the Neustadt-Perry Company of Saint Louis decided to capitalize on the fact that many Americans still wanted to build their own automobiles "Just like the Duryea Brothers." At a greatly reduced price, that company would ship all the necessary parts for its complete car — plus easy-to-follow instructions for putting it together. (Since today's automobile has some 15,000 parts, a diagram for assembling one might now be a bit more difficult to follow.)

Meanwhile, the future "master of mass production," Henry Ford, had devised a scheme to bring himself and his automobile to the attention of the American people. The scheme was simplicity itself: He built a racer and challenged the informal champion, Alexander Winton, to a 10 mile race. Winton accepted and, on October 10, 1901, the race was held on a track near Detroit. Henry Ford was the winner. His time of 13 minutes and 24 seconds brought him national acclaim. For several years thereafter, Ford kept himself and his cars in the limelight by building two more racers — the "999" and the "Arrow" — and hiring Barney Oldfield to drive them. That winning combination soon became world famous, and Henry Ford was on his way. *

From Ben Hur to the current winner of the Indianapolis International Sweepstakes, mankind has always enjoyed a race. In the days of Imperial Rome, the winners of the big chariot races became rich and famous. (While there is no specific information on the subject, it is logical to assume that the manufacturers of the winning chariots did all right too.) And so it was in the early days of the automobile industry. For example, Barney Oldfield's favorite story was about how he and Henry Ford had made each other — with Barney claiming that he did much the better job! And still today, our response to the idea of a race is so natural that even when an expectant mother fails to get to the hospital on time, the newspapers almost always use the phrase "loses race with stork."

One of the most famous sporting events of all time was the annual race for the Vanderbilt Cup. The first race covered a 30 mile course on the roads of Long Island in 1904. It was won by a French Panhard that had a top speed of 90 miles an hour. The last Vanderbilt Race, in 1916 at Santa Monica, California, was also won by a French import. In between, the sponsor twice attempted to cancel the race because of the appallingly high rates of death and injury to both drivers and spectators. But popular demand wouldn't permit it. The 1906 race attracted 300,000 spectators — the largest crowd ever to attend a sporting event in America.

*For the most part, Ford Motor Company, Fisher Body, General Motors, and Chrysler are not mentioned in this summary chapter of the automobile industry from 1900 to 1929 because each is discussed in a separate chapter.

When William K. Vanderbilt, Jr., first announced his sponsorship of the race, his hope was that the gruelling race track tests would lead to safety and mechanical improvements to the automobile in general. In addition, as a car fancier and racing driver himself, he wished to bring recognition to American cars and drivers. Both aims were accomplished, but the huge crowds seemed far more interested in the sheer excitement of the race than in "improving the breed." In some respects, the event was not entirely dissimilar from those chariot races in the Circus Maximus of old Rome.

It is obvious, of course, that speed was the objective of those races. But increased speed throughout the early history of the automobile industry brought improved engines, tires, and fuel — and more safety devices to protect the driver. Those mechanical and safety features soon appeared, in turn, on the stock commercial models. Several automobile manufacturers considered racing so important to the success of their companies that they kept a team of racing drivers permanently on their payrolls. *

But perhaps the Glidden Tours of 1905-1913 were far more successful in "improving the breed" of cars for everyday use than were all those races combined. Those tours were especially successful in calling attention to the frightful road conditions of the United States in the early 1900's. Charles J. Glidden was a wealthy "telephone" man who, after retiring from active business in 1900, became an ardent motor tourist and voluntary press-agent for the automobile. In 1904, he participated in a publicity feat that was designed to feature the thrills and pleasures of both the automobile and the Louisiana Purchase

---

*The Elgin Road Race (1900-1933) provides a side light on the influence of famous racers. In the early 1900's, no red-blooded American male would even consider wearing an "effeminate" wrist watch. But then the Elgin Watch Company began its sponsorship of that famous road race — and showed pictures of Barney Oldfield, Louis Chevrolet, Bob Burman, Eddie Rickenbacker, Ralph De Palma, Wilbur Shaw, and other racing champions wearing wrist watches! That same tried and true advertising idea is still being widely used today in various fields of merchandising. It still works wonderfully well.

Photo Courtesy G-M

First Production Model of the Cadillac, 1903

Pierce-Arrow, 1910

Photo Courtesy A.M.A.

Photo Courtesy A.M.A.

"It Will Never Replace Us Horses"

29

Mrs. John Ramsey and her three companions drove this 1909 Maxwell-Briscoe 4,200 miles from New York to San Francisco, June 9 — August 6, 1909.

Photos Courtesy A.M.A.

30

Centennial (or Saint Louis Fair). Seventy automobiles in two groups started to the Fair from Boston and New York. Sixteen days later, 50 survivors got there to participate in Automobile Day.

Mr. Glidden later equipped his English Napier automobile with a second set of wheels that could be used on railroad tracks. Accompanied by his wife, he continued on to San Francisco by "rail" on the second leg of a leisurely journey that was to take them by boat, road, and "auto rail" into 39 countries all around the world. But meanwhile, he had offered an expensive trophy to the winner of an annual tour based on that successful New York to Saint Louis trip.

The first one was held in July of 1905, over a winding route from New York City to Bretton Woods, New Hampshire and return — a total distance of 870 miles. Those Glidden Tours were not races but "controlled performance tests" run under the direction of the American Automobile Association. The winner was determined by total performance — driving skill and mechanical ability of the operator, performance of the automobile, and other criteria that varied from time to time. Percy Pierce, driving his Pierce Great Arrow, was the winner of the first Glidden Tour. The next three tours were also won by his Pierce-Arrows. An Alco was the winner of the fifth.

There was one woman driver among the 34 entries in that first Glidden Tour of 1905 — Mrs. Joan Newton Cuneo, driving a White Steamer. She was wearing the traditional feminine attire of long skirt, ample petticoats and a monstrous hat. Perhaps that was the reason why, on the first day out, she ran into another car and slipped over the edge of a small bridge into the stream below. While she wasn't injured, her car didn't fare so well. The newspapers, of course, featured both her courageous entry and her inglorious exit; it was good copy. Men readers enjoyed the story immensely; they saw the humor in it. Women readers also enjoyed the story; perhaps they detected in it a vision of the better life that the automobile was to bring to them.

Those Glidden Tours were designed strictly for amateurs. Each year, the Tour was held in a different part of the country and over various types of terrain. The primary purpose of the Tour was to publicize driving for pleasure instead of records, reliability instead of speed, practical family and business needs instead of the unusual and bizarre. In those Glidden Tours, it was usually the customers — not the manufacturers — who were using their own money to advertise the excellence of the product! Even so, those comparatively tame and leisurely tours soon declined in popularity, and disappeared — while the increasingly exciting speed races continued to attract vast crowds.

The best known of them all, and the one that still packs them in every year, is the 500 mile Memorial Day Sweepstakes at the Indianapolis Speedway. The first 500 mile race on that enclosed, two-and-one-half-mile-long, circular track in 1911 was won by Ray Harroun, driving a Marmon "Wasp" at an average speed of 74.6 miles per hour. To help him watch his competitors from all angles, Harroun installed the first rear view mirror that appeared on any American automobile. (It had been used on French cars about five years earlier.) During the race, one driver was killed and several more were injured. The 77,000 viewers of that first marathon increased to 100,000 the next year, and then steadily upward to the current 200,000 or so. There have been 48 deaths and several hundred serious injuries since the track opened in 1909.

During the 1958 race, there was a spectacular pile-up of 13 cars — and one driver was burned to death as the crowd screamed in horrified fascination. The winner of the race was Jimmy Bryan. His average speed was 133.79 miles per hour. He was driving a Belond Special — the same car in which Sam Hanks had set the all-time Indianapolis speed record of 135.6 miles per hour in winning the previous year's race.

Since the Indianapolis "500" is supposed to be the equivalent of 50,000 miles of ordinary driving, the owners and supporters of the track claim that the race still serves the purpose of testing and improving the automobile. They point to the fact that, over the years and still today, automobile tires have been improved steadily because new processes and methods had to be developed to permit them to bear up under the high speeds and stresses demanded by the race. And among the several mechanical advances that have been tested on the Speedway are high-compression engines, fuel injection, safety glass windows, Ethyl gasoline, and the French invention for independent wheel suspension.

In the early 1900's, those races, tours, and endurance contests unquestionably served a useful purpose. It was important to produce cars that would stand up under rough treatment, that could go 40 miles an hour, that were more comfortable and safer. Speed races and other contests served as the universal testing grounds for those purposes. But today, automobile manufacturers have their own specially constructed testing grounds where they can *and do* discover the complete performance characteristics of their products.

During the past 40 years, the various contests for more speed have become totally unrelated to the automobile as we know it or ever will know it. For example, the current speed record is 403 miles per hour — set by Captain George Eystron in 1947.

But because races played an important part in the development of the automobile, the highlights of various of those contests are here included in this summary of the early days of the automobile industry. For example, in 1906 a Buick won the 1,000 mile free-for-all at the Empire City track. But of far more importance, the vital need for trucks was dramatically called to the attention of Walter C. White of the White Motor Company when he was trying to ship supplies from Los Angeles to the victims of the San Francisco earthquake. (At the time, he ordered all White dealers in California to put every available vehicle at the disposal of the stricken city, and he personally led a loaded caravan of those passenger cars from Los Angeles to San Francisco.) Within a year, both White and International Harvester were producing trucks.

It was during this early period of the automobile that Carrie Nation discovered she could get even more newspaper coverage for her saloon-smashing crusade if she drove her car to the saloon she had selected to wreck. And two leading suffragettes, Alice Burke and Nell Richardson, attracted attention both to themselves and their cause by crusading by automobile. In reporting the 1906 Automobile Show, the *New York American* headlined its story: AUTO STYLES ARE CHANGING TO MEET DEMANDS OF WOMEN — THE HAND THAT ROCKS THE CRADLE HAS A LOT TO DO WITH THE SELECTION OF THE FAMILY CAR. And in 1907, Dr. Hannah Graham, a woman physician in Indianapolis, joined the increasing number of doctors who were making their house calls in an automobile instead of a horse and buggy.

An American finally won a Vanderbilt Cup — George H. Robertson, driving a Locomobile, in 1908. That race was run on the first real concrete road built in America — 11 miles long, 24 feet wide, banked curves, privately owned by the Long Island Motor Parkway Company, and open to the public on a toll basis. During the year, 61 new makes of automobiles were offered to an increasingly interested public. And various types of self-starters began to be featured by almost all car manufacturers. In 1909, more than 124,000 passenger cars were produced, plus 3,300 trucks and buses. And in 1910, the American La France Fire Engine Company offered its first motorized vehicles.

By 1911, women drivers had become so numerous that they caused little comment — other than the traditional, ever-present, and scathing masculine remarks about "women drivers," of course. But the hand-cranking of those balky monsters (especially in cold weather) seemed to remain forever beyond their powers. Then Charles F. Kettering applied his genius for electricity to the self-starter that had been invented as early as 1895.

An Early Pick-Up

Photos Courtesy A.M.A.

WORLD WAR ONE

Photos Courtesy White Motor Co.

Of the two men who deserve the most credit for turning the self-starter from an unpredictable gadget into a dependable servant, certainly Mr. Kettering should be placed first. The other man is Vincent Bendix for his invention of the "Bendix drive" coupling for electrical self-starters. Perhaps that practical self-starter in 1911, rather than a constitutional amendment in 1920, deserves a lion's share of the credit for "emancipating" women. Since it was soon followed by improved roads and the mass production of under-five-hundred-dollar automobiles, women were almost as free to travel as were men. (Today, 46 per cent of all women over 15 years of age have drivers licenses.)

Also in 1911, those famous double-decker buses first appeared on Fifth Avenue. And later on that year, the U. S. Court of Appeals decreed that Henry Ford and others had not infringed upon George B. Selden's patent for a gasoline automobile. Freed from that threat of patent monopoly, the industry produced 200,000 passenger cars and 11,000 trucks and buses during the year. And the real commercial possibilities of the truck were vividly dramatized the following year when a Packard truck carried a three-ton pay load from New York to San Francisco in 46 days.

In 1914, more than 400 different automobile manufacturers were in business. They produced more than a half-million passenger cars.

Along about this time, Model T Ford jokes began sweeping the country. Henry Ford's personal favorite concerned a man's death-bed request that his Model T be buried with him because he had never yet been in a hole it couldn't get him out of. Throughout this period, those hundreds of automobile manufacturers were also searching frantically for some slogan that might catch the public eye. Among the many thousands of efforts were, "He who looks before he leaps, buys a Blair and buys for keeps" and "Buy a Bates and keep your dates."

When the nation went to war in 1917, all car and truck

manufacturers automatically offered their full services and facilities to the government. The industry quickly began turning out vast quantities of shells, depth bombs, airplane bombs, torpedo directors, airplane bodies and parts, tractors, tanks, and guns. In November of 1918, the automobile industry was producing 1,000 Liberty airplane engines a week — and Ford had the Eagle submarine chaser in quantity production. By the end of the war, 92,000 trucks had been shipped to Europe — plus many more thousands of cars for ambulance and staff work. Lord Curzon of the British War Cabinet said that the war could not have been won without the motor vehicles and other materials produced by the automobile industry. Actually, the full potential of the lusty young automobile giant for war production was just beginning to be realized when the conflict ended.

This subject of the automobile industry and armament production is discussed more fully in the next chapter. It is sufficient here merely to record the additional fact that the part played by the internal combustion engine (on wheels and in the air) during World War One gave birth to an entirely new concept of war tactics. While it was not realized at the time, the idea of mechanized "blitzkrieg" was born in 1914 when about 4,000 French reserve troops were packed into 700 taxicabs and rushed from Paris to the Marne to attack the flank of the advancing German cavalry and foot soldiers.

(Apparently, that unexpected feat so astounded the Germans that the Von Schlieffen Plan to end the war in a hurry was thrown off schedule long enough to permit a reorganization of the retreating and seemingly demoralized allied armies.) The appearance of the tank in 1916, and the increasing use of the airplane in the last two years of the war, merely confirmed the fact that a new form of warfare had arrived.

The industry quickly reconverted from war production and, in 1919, produced almost two million cars and trucks. From 1920 to 1925, well over 200 new automobiles were introduced to the American public. Among them were the Chrysler, Rickenbacker, Star, and Wills Sainte Claire. Production of cars and trucks passed the four million mark in 1923. And in 1925, the production of closed cars finally exceeded the production of open models — from 10 percent in 1919 to 90 percent in 1929.

The closed automobile body (first used in France in 1902) was of vital importance to the American people and the way we live. When the closed car was offered at a price comparable to the open car, the seasonal nature of automobile making and selling was over. The car was thereby converted from a fair-weather luxury into a year-around necessity. The automobile industry as we know it today was in full swing.

Chapter 3
IF WAR SHOULD COME...

In 1957, the number of cars *stolen* in the United States was greater than the number of cars *produced* in Russia — 264,000 versus 113,600. While the figure for car thefts in the Soviet Union is unavailable, it automatically has to be lower than our own. The figure for car thefts among the head-hunters of Central New Guinea is also exceedingly low.

Be that as it may, the fact that more than twice as many passenger cars are stolen in the U. S. as are produced in the U. S. S. R. does suggest the vast difference between the productivity of the economic systems of the two countries.

The communist officials have always been exceedingly sensitive about their inferior record of production and the resulting subsistence level of living in Russia. They have often gone to great lengths to persuade their people that communism is more productive economically — and more desirable socially — than the free market and the free ballot. From 1930 through 1940, their chief propaganda weapon for that purpose was the depression and the resulting human suffering in the United States. To help develop that theme, they imported a few American movies based on the worst features of that sad decade. But even though the communists selected only the most distorted or extreme examples to show to their people, the results were sometimes the reverse of what they had in mind. According to popular report, "The Grapes of Wrath" was one such movie that backfired.

When the Russian people saw that depression movie about jobless, homeless, and hungry Americans, they were supposed to become convinced that they themselves were indeed fortunate to be living under a communist system. But instead, their general reaction was one of envy — for they saw that even the "poorest" family in America owned a truck! They saw that family load its meager possessions on the truck and travel across half a continent to hunt for work in another state. And that poorest family in the depths of the depression still had enough money to buy the gas and food to get there.

The overwhelming majority of the Russian people had far less money, food, clothing, and furniture than even those poorest Americans during that distressing period, and none of them owned a truck. Even if they had, their government forbade them to leave their villages and to travel around Russia to look for a job. Thus the movie only deepened the conviction of many Russians that capitalist America was still the promised land to which so many of their fellow-countrymen had migrated before the communists abolished their freedom to leave. Needless to say, the movie was soon withdrawn from circulation.

True enough, the 1930-1940 depression brought great suffering to the American people. Thirteen million were out of work in 1933. As late as 1940, there were still around nine million unemployed. Industry, of course, suffered in proportion. The automobile industry was especially hard hit after its previous 30 years of almost uninterrupted progress and prosperity.

From 1900 to 1930, more than 45 million cars, trucks, and buses had been produced in the United States. In 1929, production of automobiles and trucks was well over five million — 4.6 million passenger cars and 771,000 trucks and buses. During the five years from 1925 to 1930, about 75 new makes of cars had been introduced. They included the Graham-Paige, Durant, La Salle, and Cord. A national "drive yourself" chain was established, the Aerocar house trailer made its appearance, coast-to-coast bus service was inaugurated, and diesel powered trucks began to serve as the work horses of America. The catchy slogan, "Two cars in every garage," was heard with increasing frequency.

Then came 1930. Production of cars and trucks dropped to less than half of the previous year's record. In 1931, '32 and '33, production dropped still lower. In 1934, '35, '36 and '37, automobile production began a slow but steady climb. Then, in

1938, it dropped back to the 1930 level. During those eight years, the rate of failure among automobile producers was exceptionally high. For awhile, the mighty giant was sick unto death. But beginning in 1939, the automobile industry surged rapidly upward to heights then undreamed of.

The communists have long alleged that the capitalist economy must have constant wars in order to survive. They continue to make that vicious statement even though they are well aware that it was *war itself* that destroyed the growing capitalism of Russia and permitted the communists to seize power. The wars of this century have severely restricted (and in some cases, completely abolished) the private accumulation and ownership of capital all over the world. But in spite of that undisputed fact, millions of otherwise sane people still parrot the communist line that capitalism (private ownership) *thrives* on war! The truth, of course, is just the reverse. The highest profit years for the big automobile manufacturers (as well as for the large industrial companies in general) have consistently occurred during years when the United States was at peace.

Soon after the death of Stalin in Russia, a slight crack appeared in the customary communist line. For example, in his public speeches, Premier Khrushchev began to admit that the people of the capitalist west (especially those in the United States) might actually have a higher level of living than those of the socialist east. He exhorted his people to work harder and to save more, so they too could have better housing, clothing, and food within a few more years. But even as he admitted that the capitalist nations are ahead of Russia in their production of consumer goods and services, Khrushchev proudly boasted that the communists are leading in the production of armaments. Aside from what that boast does to the communist line that it is *capitalism* that gears its economy to armaments, there is also serious doubt as to its accuracy.

It is possible, of course, that an all-out war between Russia and the United States would be over in a matter of hours —

with a hundred million or so people in both nations destroyed by atomic blasts and the resulting fall-out. In that case, the few survivors would hardly be interested in arguing the relative merits of the two types of economy. But if the war were to last long enough to be decided by *total* productivity, the odds would be overwhelmingly in our favor. Perhaps a brief examination of the record of the automotive industry during World War Two might be of considerable help in visualizing that fact.

In his glowing tribute to "Detroit" in 1946, General Dwight D. Eisenhower was doubtless merely using that handy name as a symbol of the contribution that American industry in general had made to the war effort. For obviously, the contribution of Detroit would have been largely ineffective without the oil and rubber industries, without the fantastic quantities of food produced on our farms, without the ship builders, the steel makers, the airplane companies, and a host of others. But General Eisenhower was referring specifically to the automobile industry when he said, "Detroit, that to most of us before the war meant only trucks and automobiles, came to mean, in war, practically everything we needed to defeat the enemy. Every man in our Armed Forces who marched or rode or sailed or flew into combat was armed and equipped to an appreciable extent by this city." Here follows a summary of the story behind that remark.

In May of 1940, President Roosevelt asked William S. Knudsen to leave his job as president of General Motors and come to Washington to organize and direct the nation's rearmament program as head of the Office of Production Management. Mr. Knudsen unhesitatingly accepted the opportunity to be of assistance to his adopted country.

In September of that year, Knudsen attended the board meeting of the Automobile Manufacturers Association in New York. His purpose was to explain to those men the desperate position of the British forces and our own appalling lack of preparedness, especially in the air. Since the United States was

Normandy Beachhead

Deep in Germany

Photos Courtesy U.S. Army

Photos Courtesy U.S. Army

Savenna River, Italy

46

not then at war, he could only ask their voluntary cooperation in a program to remedy that situation. But Mr. Knudsen knew his men; their cooperation was instantaneous and complete.

Ten days later, the representatives of more than a hundred manufacturers of automotive products and parts met in Detroit and organized the Automotive Committee for Air Defense. The famed General "Jimmy" Doolittle (then a major) was technical advisor.

In the summer of 1941, the Society of Automotive Engineers sponsored the War Engineering Board to pool the facilities of the entire industry's laboratories for war work. And within a few days after Pearl Harbor, the total automotive industry was voluntarily organized into the Automotive Council for War Production, with Packard's Alvan Macauley as president. There was no "czar" over the industry; none was needed to secure the maximum cooperation and production from the automobile manufacturers. Mr. Macauley mostly performed the clearinghouse function of coordinating toward a common objective the voluntary efforts of men who had so recently been fierce competitors. But now all machines, plants, patents, personnel — all resources of any nature — were pooled for the common objective of victory. If the automobile men themselves were not surprised at the results, certainly the Germans and Japanese were! Here follows a summary of the contribution made to the war effort by the automotive industry.

During the two years before the United States was officially at war, all of the automobile companies were beginning war production of some sort. In 1940, Dodge was building special trucks — and White Motor Company was building scout cars — for the U. S. Army. Packard started to build Rolls-Royce aircraft engines, and Ford began building Pratt and Whitney aircraft engines.

During 1941, Buick built an entirely new aviation engine plant. Oldsmobile began producing shells. Pontiac began work on the Oerlikon anti-aircraft gun. And various other divisions of General Motors were producing machine guns. Chrysler began the mass production of tanks — from a completely new factory that had been designed, built, and tooled within seven months after K. T. Keller and his associates were shown a model of the tank the Army wanted. Chrysler also completed its first anti-aircraft gun. Ford Motor Company began producing combat cars, and started building its famed Willow Run plant for aircraft production. Willys delivered its first Jeeps. White was producing half-tracks, tank destroyers, and cargo trucks. Studebaker began the production of aircraft engines. All this was going on while the industry was steadily increasing its regular production of cars and trucks for civilian use. Thus, when war came, all of the automobile companies had already gained some experience in the production of armaments.

In December of 1943, the Automotive Council for War Production announced that 1,038 automotive plants of all categories had so far produced $13 billion worth of war materials. In February of 1944, figures were released showing that the "Detroit region" was responsible for 13.6 per cent of the nation's total production for war. In December of 1944, the Automotive Council announced that the industry had produced $9 billion worth of armaments during the year, and that the cost to the government had been reduced by one-third of the 1941 price. Also in December, it was revealed that the United States had supplied Russia with more than 345,000 motor vehicles, plus comparably large quantities of other war materials. (Total U. S. war aid to Russia exceeded $11 billion, plus extensive United Nations Relief and Rehabilitation aid after the war).

During the war, the automotive industry supplied the Armed Forces with all armored cars of all types. It also produced 87 per cent of all aircraft bombs, 75 per cent of all aircraft engines and 50 per cent of all Diesel engines, 10 per cent of completed airplanes, 85 per cent of the steel helmets, 57 per cent of all tanks, 47 per cent of the machine guns and 56 per cent of the carbines, 10 per cent of the torpedoes, 10 per cent of the land mines and 3 per cent of the marine mines. In addition, the automotive industry also produced huge quantities of such things as gyrocompasses, automatic pilots, mess kits, tent heaters, range finders, bomb sights — and several billion rounds of small-caliber cartridges.

By the end of the war, the automotive industry had delivered $29 billion worth of war products. That was about 20 per cent of the national output for that category. As General Eisenhower said in 1946, "The weapons of war came to us in the field in such numbers that the Allies were able to bury the enemy under weight of metal. . . . We were in a position to sacrifice metal to save American lives." In that statement can be found the real meaning of "Detroit" as a symbol of our industrial production for war; it permits us to expend metal instead of American lives.

Along with the above production record, the automotive industry also had to produce the parts necessary to keep in service the motor vehicles already in existence. If anyone still had any doubt that the automobile was a necessity instead of a luxury, that doubt was soon dispelled with the coming of war. Millions of people literally had to have them in order to get to and from their jobs that were essential to the war effort. When production of automobiles for civilian use was stopped in early 1942, there were about 33 million cars, trucks, and buses registered in the United States. At that point, some short-sighted planners in Washington seriously curtailed the production of parts that would be necessary to keep those vehicles in service for essential uses and personnel — doctors, war workers, farmers, nurses, firemen, policemen, teachers, and so on. Fortunately, better thinking soon recognized the fact that parts production should be *increased* over customary and former levels, since there were not going to be any more cars and trucks to replace those that would have to be junked for lack of replacement parts. The proper permission was given, and the automotive industry produced the necessary parts to keep our civilian motor fleet in running order for essential services throughout the war. The value of parts and accessories produced rose steadily from $553 million in 1940 to over one billion dollars in 1945.

As far as the American motorist who already owned a car was concerned, the war ended on August 14, 1945. On that day, gasoline rationing ended — and the joyous cry, "Fill 'er up," was again heard throughout the land. (Thirteen years later the 25 service stations in Moscow were finally permitted to sell gasoline without rationing coupons to the 28,000 privately owned cars in the Soviet capital that contained some five million people.) From the same viewpoint, the war had already started to end for the automobile industry on the previous July 1, when the manufacturers were permitted to begin retooling for civilian production. But unfinished war contracts, plus reconversion and labor problems, permitted only 69,532 passenger cars to be produced before the year was out. During 1946, however, more than three million cars and trucks were produced for a clamoring public that wanted to buy between 15 and 20 millions of them at once.

The next year, production reached almost five million — plus the staggering total of $2.35 billion worth of replacement parts. In 1948, production went over the five million mark — including the one-hundred-millionth motor vehicle built in the United States. The following year, production jumped to almost 6.3 million cars, trucks, and buses. And in 1950, it soared over the eight million mark. In June of that year, in Korea, we went to war again.

Once more, the automotive industry began turning out armaments in huge quantities. The managers and employees of the various companies were now thoroughly familiar with the process. And they were generally able to supply the Armed Forces with whatever they wanted, while continuing to produce millions of passenger cars for the seemingly insatiable civilian demand — 5.3 million passenger cars in 1951, and 4.3 million the following year.

In 1955, the industry produced the all-time record of 9,169,-

Tankdozer versus Japanese Pillbox

Photos Courtesy U.S. Army

Malimba River, Guadalcanal

51

Korea

Photos Courtesy U.S. Army

276 cars, trucks, and buses. At the same time, it was continuing to produce vast quantities of armaments for the Armed Forces in our continuing "cold war" with Russia. Meanwhile the entire Russian automotive industry produced a total of only 445,300 cars, trucks, and buses for that year.

If the Russian leaders fully understood the actual and potential productive capacity of our automotive and other industries for both war and peace, it is doubtful that they would ever deliberately challenge us to a head-on clash. But in spite of some recent evidence to the contrary, there is still grave doubt that they do really understand it. For example, you are doubtless familiar with the story of the reaction of the visiting Russian officials in Detroit when they saw the crowded parking lots around the various automobile plants. They assumed that those cars belonged to the owners and managers of the factories — as would be the case in their own country. Thus they expressed the opinion that the plants obviously couldn't be very efficient if that many bosses were needed to run them. They refused to believe that those thousands of magnificent automobiles belonged to the men who were working on the assembly lines. They just laughed at that explanation because they had been taught that it couldn't possibly be true.

We would be foolish indeed to assume that the Russians doubt their own propaganda. They honestly believe that we would like to destroy them. And they further believe that, if war comes, they can destroy us. We, in turn, are firmly convinced that the Russian communist leaders plan to conquer the world. And further, we are confident that we can stop them militarily, if it comes to that. Thus we must face this harsh fact: As long as those diametrically opposed beliefs continue to exist, there can be no real peace. Since we seem destined to continue to live under an armed truce of uncertain and precarious duration, we are fortunate indeed that our automotive industry is now designed to produce with equal ease vast quantities of weapons for war or automobiles for peace.

Chapter 4
FROM THE CRADLE TO THE GRAVE

According to tradition, a baby's first word is supposed to be "mama." But the first clear and distinct word uttered by this writer's son was "car." Perhaps it was because he had an excellent view of the street from his dressing table and play pen, and his parents entertained him by pointing at the passing automobiles and saying, "See the big car." His first conscious effort to distinguish between red and black came from watching and identifying automobiles. And his first rational idea of danger was derived from the constant drilling of his parents on the subject of streets and cars. That first word was truly appropriate — for as long as he lives, it is certain that an automobile will play a vital part in all his activities. He had his first automobile ride at the age of five days when he came home from the maternity hospital. The chances are that he'll ride to school in a car or bus. Surely he will do a large part of his courting in a car — and will share it with his bride on their honeymoon. In one way or another, the automobile will necessarily play an important part in his business career. And when he dies, his journey to the cemetery will also be by motor vehicle.

Doubtless, you are well aware of the importance of the automobile in the way we live. Since you probably own one, you hardly need to read a book to find that out! But even so, it's highly doubtful that most people actually do realize just how vital the automobile and the automotive industry have become to our daily activities — to our economy, our social life, and even our government.

First and most important, machines of all types are today supplying the equivalent energy of about 800 strong men for every person in the United States. And those "mechanical slaves" will happily work 24 hours every day when needed. Some wag once wryly joked, "Not only did the machine free the slaves — why, it even freed the horses!" And in a manner of speaking, so it did. With all that cheap mechanical horsepower available, the flesh and blood originals just couldn't compete. More than 90 per cent of that mechanical horsepower is supplied by our automobiles, trucks, buses, and tractors. Now let's briefly examine a few of the specific results of that development in our daily lives.

Start with yourself and the most obvious example of all: How do you get to work? In 1957, almost 68 per cent of us went by private automobile. (And for the most part, even those of us who used public transportation rode a bus — or a train pulled by a Diesel engine that was manufactured by an automobile company!)

There's a one in seven chance that the job you're going to depends directly on the manufacture, distribution, service, or use of motor vehicles. An unknown (but certainly still greater) number of jobs are indirectly affected by motor transportation — doctors, salesmen, migratory workers, schools, forestry, shopping centers, restaurants and, to varying extents, almost any other job or industry you care to mention. If there were no automotive industry, about 700,000 businesses (or almost one of each six businesses now in existence) would be gone — along with the more than 10.3 million jobs that are now directly dependent on "highway transportation" in one form or another.

Most of those jobs are among the highest paying in the nation. In automobile manufacturing, wages average 22 per cent higher than the average for "all manufacturing" in the United States. In rubber, the figure is 26 per cent higher — and in petroleum, 30 per cent higher. The jobs and wages provided by the airlines and railroads are also heavily dependent on the automotive industry that manufactures so many of the engines and parts used by those forms of transportation. To a lesser but still important extent, all forms of water transportation look to the automobile companies for engines and parts. (They also look to them for considerable business, such as the 373,000 cars, trucks, and buses we exported in 1957; and the 273,000 we imported.)

The best customer of the steel companies is, of course, "highway transportation," including the building of the roads themselves. But the vital part played by the automotive industry in our daily lives is perhaps most dramatically illustrated by our dependence on it for our food.

The story of farming and the automobile is told in the next chapter. Here it is enough to point out that modern farming is absolutely dependent on tractors, trucks, combines, and similar machines manufactured by the automotive industry. And when the food is produced, about 90 per cent of it goes to market by highway. As a result, we city dwellers today are completely dependent upon the products of the automotive industry for the growing and transporting of our daily food. We also look to it for our fire engines, fuel trucks, police cars, snow removal equipment, sanitation trucks, ambulances, and so on. City life as it is lived today could not possibly have developed without the internal combustion engine on wheels.

Outside of the cities, we 40 million or so suburbanites have also based our way of life on the automobile. Without it, we could never have built those millions of wonderful homes out in Sunshine Acres or Fresh Air Heights. Imagine trying to raise a family in the suburbs without milk trucks, bakery trucks, laundry trucks, fuel trucks, parcel delivery trucks, mail trucks, grocery delivery trucks, garbage trucks, paper delivery trucks, ambulances and doctors' cars, school buses, repairmen's trucks, dry cleaning trucks, and the other motor vehicles that make deliveries of various kinds to your door. Imagine not having even a *first* car to jump into for a fast trip to those convenient out-of-town shopping centers and super markets!

In short, modern suburban living is completely dependent on the automotive industry — not only for transportation but, to a considerable extent, for refrigerators, stoves, heating and cooling equipment, washers, dryers, bicycles, sporting equipment, and so on. Without the automobile industry, most of the 25 per cent of us who now live in suburban areas would have to crowd ourselves back into the towns and cities — or along the street car and railroad tracks — as was necessarily the case before the automobile came along. The current problem of parking space for cars is indeed serious, but it is not even remotely as serious as the pre-automobile problem of living space for children. Unquestionably, our children profited most of all when the automobile made it possible for us to live in the suburbs while commuting to our jobs in the city.

True enough, even if we lived in cities without automobiles, most of us would still try to take trips out of them by whatever conveyances were available, as did our parents and grandparents before us. For we are a traveling people. Actually, thousands and thousands of Americans have been born while their parents were making a trip. Sometimes it was on a ship when the parents were immigrating to the United States. Sometimes it was in a covered wagon while the parents were struggling westward in one of those famous prairie schooners. Sometimes it was on a river boat or a steam-driven train. (Nowadays, many of the children among the three million people who live in one million trailers are quite scornful about houses that have no wheels.) Travel is in our blood; if it hadn't been, there wouldn't even be a United States.

Even our appeals to patriotism are often based on our love of travel! The slogan, "Join the Navy and see the world," is far more in harmony with our nature than is the plea, "Uncle Sam needs you." The record is clear that we will fight if we must, but we want a handy foreign language phrase book issued along with the rifle. While we soldiers were only joking when we referred to our "all expenses paid, vacation trip abroad," the joke still indicated that we considered ourselves tourists as well as soldiers. The record is conclusive, however, that we prefer to pay our own way in our own automobiles — with a camera instead of a gun.

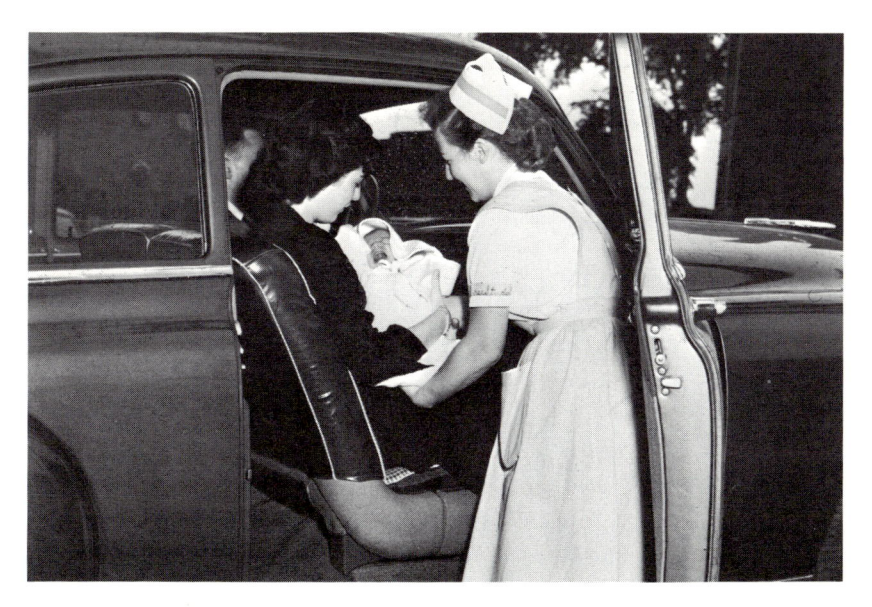

Photo Courtesy A.M.A.

Photo Courtesy Chrysler Corp.

Photo Courtesy G-M

Photo Courtesy Paramount Photo Studio
Huntington Woods, Mich.

60

Almost 80 million of us had operators' licenses in 1957. And more than 73 per cent of American families then owned one or more automobiles. (Almost 13 per cent of us owned two or more.) Excluding all military vehicles, there were 68.5 million cars, trucks, and buses registered in the United States in 1957. (Bumper to bumper, they would form a line well over 200,000 miles long.) We drove them a total distance of 643 *billion* miles over our 3.5 million miles of roads and streets, while consuming more than 52 billion gallons of motor fuel and 107 million gallons of antifreeze. Passenger cars accounted for well over 500 billion miles of that incomprehensible total.

A large portion of those miles were driven by the four out of five families that take their vacations by car. The combined records of our 27 largest national parks show that 20.3 million of us in six million cars were visitors in 1957 — Yellowstone, Grand Canyon, the Great Smokies, Mammoth Cave, and so on over the length and breadth of the nation. The Army Engineer recreation areas and the U. S. Forest Service reported well over 100 million visitors during the year. Something like 11 billion miles were traveled on hunting and fishing trips. Our Canadian and Mexican neighbors doubtless sometimes suspect that most Americans who own cars have driven them across the border for a visit. And an increasing number of us are shipping the car along with the trunk when we set out to see Europe.

The "vacation industry" in the United States is absolutely dependent on the automobile. In more than half of our states, that industry ranks among the top three. In New Jersey, New Mexico, and Florida the tourist business tops the list. All of our resorts depend on the automobile to some considerable extent, and many of them wouldn't have even one guest without it. By 1957, the automobile had brought into existence some 34,000 motels, tourist courts, and trailer parks — and some 4,700 drive-in movies, as well as a few hundred summer theatres and music festivals. The tens-of-thousands of home owners who still accommodate overnight guests have built their modest businesses on the automobile. And, of course, the owners and employees of some 450 automobile race tracks understandably look with favor upon the automobile industry — as do the persons whose jobs depend on the printing and distributing of 300 million giveaway road maps each year. Finally, the high value of many of those magnificent beaches in Florida, California, Virginia, and most other states is based solidly on the availability of the automobile. Without it, they would again become merely barren stretches of uninhabited and valueless sand.

It has long been claimed that our educational system is responsible for welding America's diversified peoples into one nation. True enough, a common educational background does serve that purpose. But reading about how other people live is not nearly so effective as actually traveling among them. The automobile — and the automobile alone — has made that possible on a large scale. We easterners no longer merely read about rodeos or see them only in movies; millions of us get in our cars and drive west to watch them in action. The New Englander is convinced that he has been exposed to another language — as well as to another way of life — when he heads his car back north from his trip to South Carolina. While the far-westerner may display his P. C. D. P. sticker (Pacific Coast Displaced Person) when he drives east, at least he learns how the other half lives. A Texan, viewing that spot from where a shot was heard around the world, may not dress or think quite like his Massachusetts compatriots — but the fact remains that he has driven a mighty long way to satisfy his desire to actually stand on the ground that is as hallowed to him as the Alamo.

Before the automobile, we often depended on the Sunday evening lecturer with his illustrated slides to tell us about the peoples, problems, and terrain of our vast nation. Now we pack the kids in the back seat and head north, east, south, and west to see for ourselves — and to take our own billions of travel pictures. Our children (along with their parents) cannot help but be impressed by the varied peoples and resources they meet and see as they drive around the United States. Perhaps the trips are fast — and, admittedly, they are frequently superficial — but even so, it's still better than merely reading about our triumphs and tragedies in a book. We are not yet "one people in thought and act" (pray God we never will be), but those millions of yearly inter-sectional visits do give us some idea of how our fellow-Americans work, play, and attempt to settle their own particular problems — be they industrial, racial, or geographical. We thereby learn first-hand that those problems are seldom as simple as the demagogues would have us believe. Surely such knowledge makes us better people and better Americans. Without the automobile, that superior type of education just wouldn't be possible for most of us. Thomas A. Edison had that fact in mind when he said, "The great value of the automobile is not the fact that it has made it easier and quicker and cheaper to go places, but the fact that it has inspired several million people to go."

From 1900 through 1957, the American automotive industry produced 166 million cars, trucks, and buses — with a total value of more than $176 billion, excluding all federal excise taxes. How many hundreds of billions of dollars in taxes have resulted from the sale and use of those vehicles is not known. But recent yearly taxes derived from "highway transportation" will offer some idea of the magnitude of governmental income from that source. For example, $8.8 billion was collected by *special* motor vehicle taxes in 1957 — federal excise taxes on automobiles and fuels, tolls, specific local taxes, registration fees, and state gasoline taxes. That figure does not include the $1.82 billion paid in direct federal, state, and local taxes in 1957 by General Motors (exclusive of all excise taxes), nor the hundreds of millions paid by the various other automobile manufacturers.

Nor does that almost $9 billion special tax include the taxes paid by the more than 43,000 franchised automobile dealers who had invested about $5 billion in their businesses that employed around 700,000 persons in 1957. Nor does it include the taxes paid by more than 182,000 filling stations and almost 19,000 auto supply shops that, along with those dealers, sold $53 billion worth of automobiles, parts, and fuel during the year. The total taxes paid by some 87,000 independent repair shops is unknown. And, of course, there is no possible way to estimate the *personal* income taxes paid by the employees of those small businesses, plus the employees of related businesses such as parking lots, map makers, taxicab and bus companies, terminal and trucking companies, auto laundries, car rental agencies, and so on. Nor is there any way to determine the federal and state taxes paid on the dividends received by millions of Americans who have invested their savings in the automotive and related industries.

That almost $9 billion direct tax on motor vehicles also does not include taxes paid by the banks and finance companies that extended $16.7 billion in credit for the purchase of automobiles in 1957, or taxes from the insurance companies that handled $4.5 billion in premiums from automobile insurance in 1956. It would be difficult to estimate how much of the taxes paid by newspapers, magazines, and radio and television companies came from the more than $200 million of motor vehicle advertising in 1956. Nor do we have a proportionate tax figure for the manufacturers of the vast quantities of materials and equipment produced for the automobile in 1957 — 107 million rubber tires, 52 billion gallons of gasoline, 44 per cent of all sheet steel, 32 million batteries, 5.5 million radios, 400 million pounds of textiles for upholstery, and vast quantities of clocks, glass, chemicals, electrical equipment, lead, nickel, machine tools, and so on.

One might guess that total taxes originating from "highway transportation" in all its many ramifications could be even as much as 25 per cent of all state and federal taxes now collected. But since it is impossible to know, for example, how much of the income tax of restaurant employees should be allocated to

Photo Courtesy White Motor Co.

Photo Courtesy A.M.A.

65

Photo Courtesy White Motor Co.

Photo Courtesy Miller Meteor Co.

66

automobile customers — or what percentage of a doctor's income could logically be credited to the availability of his car — that figure must necessarily remain a questionable guess.

We don't have to guess, however, at the fact that 24 cents of every dollar spent for the purchase of automobiles is for taxes — $600 of the price of a $2,500 car in 1957 went to the government. Of total *state* tax revenues, 29 per cent comes from taxes on motor vehicle fuels and licenses. In Nebraska and New Jersey, almost half comes from those two sources. When Oregon levied the first modest gasoline tax of one cent a gallon in 1919, no one then dreamed of the vital part that taxes on motor fuel would come to play in state finances. In 1957, California raised over $297 million from its tax of six cents on a gallon of gasoline. In 14 other states, the tax per gallon was higher than six cents. Actually, it is impossible (and probably meaningless) to attempt to estimate the total taxes resulting from the automobile in *all* its uses. It is enough to say that the loss of that source of taxation would result in financial chaos and the collapse of our economy as we know it today. As a *New York Times* report on May 25, 1958 phrased it: "For all this nation's vaunted industrial diversification, this one key industry has an almost controlling effect on the economy."

The importance of the automobile in the lives of our children has already been mentioned. But perhaps the primary reason that they were featured ahead of their mothers is because the mothers prefer it that way — for it is unquestionably true that the automobile has also brought vast improvements into the economic and social lives of women.

From the very beginning of the automobile, women began to look upon it as the answer to their prayers for a convenient and economical way to visit their neighbors and relatives, to go to the city to shop, to enjoy an evening or a Sunday drive in the country, to participate in a more enjoyable social life — in short, to have a few brief respites from the brutalizing sameness of the lives that so many of them led. The mass-produced and low-priced automobile served that purpose well. But even more, both the car and the industry played a vital part in bringing another type of freedom to women — freedom to earn their own livelihoods without being absolutely at the mercy of the whims of man.

By 1900, the number of women who were working in offices and factories was already in the millions. But it was still frowned upon as an insult to the men folks; for people might think that the father or husband couldn't support them. Regardless of such social disapproval, they continued to pour into the factories and offices. By 1910, almost seven million women were employed in the United States. By 1930, the figure had risen to nearly 11 million. In 1955, about 21 million women (more than one-third of all women over 14 years of age) were working at a job for pay. In the "automotive and equipment" industry, 15 per cent of all employees were women. (It had exceeded 25 per cent during World War Two.)

But perhaps the *indirect* influence of the automobile in bettering the lives of women is more important by far than the direct jobs it provides them. Examples of that influence are found throughout this study — more jobs and better wages for husbands and fathers, improved farming and better food, access to better schools and medical service, better sanitation, vacations, suburban living, labor-saving appliances for the kitchen, and so on through scores of necessities, conveniences, and comforts that couldn't possibly have come into existence without the automobile. Perhaps among the improvements should be listed the more comfortable and practical clothing for women that developed along with the automobile. Perhaps not. Automobile or no automobile, women's clothing styles seem always to be changing anyway.

In their monumental study of how the people lived in "Middletown," in the mid-1920's, the Lynds asked hundreds of persons for their ideas about what event or development had exercised the most influence on the way people lived in that city.

Some talked about government. Others mentioned electricity, education, religion, and so on. The shortest reply was offered by an old man who had originally come to that section of the country by oxcart. He said he could summarize all the important changes that had occurred in his lifetime in just four letters, "A-U-T-O."

In those four letters, he reached the same conclusion as the Hoover Research Committee on Social Trends during the 1920's and early 1930's: "It is probable that no invention of such far-reaching importance was ever diffused with such rapidity or so quickly exerted influences that ramified the national culture, transforming even habits of thought and language."

Chapter 5

MEANWHILE, BACK ON THE FARM ...

Do you remember the good old days? Of course you do, since the good old days generally refer to whatever existed a few years ago. Apparently, it was almost always wonderful.

For example, veterans derive a peculiar pleasure from reminiscing about the good old days when they were being shot at. Successful business and professional men enjoy reliving in imagination their earlier days when they were jobless and didn't know where their next meal was coming from. Escapees from city slums often rhapsodize about those good old days when they were snitching apples and baiting cops. But of all the good old day categories, probably more nostalgic nonsense has been spoken and written about life on the pre-automobile farm than any other.

Actually, life on the farms of the United States before 1900 was a generally harsh existence. The entire family usually worked from dawn to dusk for six days every week, plus a half day of chores on Sunday. Social life and contact with the outside world were severely limited by bad roads and poor transportation. Vacations were rare or non-existent. In most cases, children were put to work just as soon as they were physically able to chop down a weed or milk a cow. At best, education was always severely limited, and sometimes there weren't any schools at all. There was little income with which to buy conveniences and comforts; stark necessity was the general rule of purchase. Sickness, accident, and death were frequent visitors. The nearest doctor was many hours away, if available at all. It was a generally lonely and undesirable life, and the farmers themselves were well aware of its shortcomings. But what could they do?

Well, there wasn't too much they could do about it — until automobiles, tractors, trucks, and other similar machines were offered to them at the low prices they could afford to pay. Then they could do plenty. And they did.

The most startling thing they did was summarized by the President in his 1958 farm message to Congress: "A century ago, an American farm worker fed himself and three others. Today he feeds himself and twenty others. A century ago, our population was 82 per cent rural. Today it is only one-third rural, and only 12 per cent of our population actually live on farms. Farm production per man hour has doubled since 1940. There has been more change in agriculture within the lifetime of men now living than in the previous two thousand years."

Of course, that fantastic improvement in farm production was not due to automotive equipment alone. A vital part has been played by new vaccines and new techniques in animal husbandry, better fertilizers and seeds, improved farming and marketing methods, weed killers, insecticides, sprays, plant hormones — and even radio-isotopes. But the fact remains that new and improved automotive machines deserve the lion's share of the credit.

In 1900, only a dozen or so farmers owned cars. There weren't *any* gasoline tractors or trucks on the farms. About 20 million horses and mules pulled the plows, wagons, and primitive reapers. By 1910, farmers owned 50,000 cars and 1,000 tractors. There still weren't any trucks for farm use.

The Department of Agriculture estimated that, in 1957, farmers owned 4.3 million cars, 2.9 million trucks, 4.6 million tractors, and unnumbered millions of special engines and vehicles that enable them to produce more in less time and at less cost. Many of those tractors are equipped with self-starters and power steering. In addition to its ordinary field work, the modern tractor has attachments for pumping, lifting, digging, sawing, arc-welding, spraying, and other types of work. Today's trucks are also most versatile in their uses. The horsepower supplied by the 20 million horses and mules on the farms of 1900 has increased to around one billion "mechani-

Photo Courtesy Ford Motor Co.

Photo Courtesy A.M.A.

73

Photo Courtesy Massey-Ferguson Co.

Photo Courtesy A.M.A.

cal" horses today. And the trend is steadily upward.

For the long-range future, certainly one of the most significant contributions made by automotive machines on the farm is this: The number of horses and mules has steadily declined from its 1925 peak of 25 million down to about 3.6 million in 1957. It is estimated that the amount of land needed to feed one horse can be used to feed four persons. Thus, millions of acres of land that were once used to grow food for animals are now available to grow food for humans.

With their machines (and egged on by government price supports), the American farmers now produce so much food that it is politically embarrassing. In an effort to stop it without displeasing the farmers, the government sometimes pays them to destroy their crops. At other times it pays them not to produce crops. Still the surplus food accumulates. The government buys the surplus and stores it away in caves, tents, ships, buildings, and even on the open ground. But the flow of food from our mechanized farms continues to increase. The government gives it away or sells it at distressed prices. But the surplus grows. There is no end in sight.

As a result, we have this strange development: Throughout history, untold millions of human beings have starved to death. Thirty years ago, millions of Russians were dying because they didn't have enough to eat. In your lifetime, famines have swept across India, China, and other nations. Even today — tonight — millions of persons will still go to bed hungry. But in the United States, the present administration may be voted out of office unless it devises a politically acceptable scheme to make food more scarce! While that may sound somewhat Alice-in-wonderlandish, you need only read your daily paper to confirm it.

The problem of how to dispose of our surplus food has now become a purely political issue. Thus it is outside the scope of this study. We are here primarily concerned with the part played by the automotive industry in *increasing* the farmer's productive power and helping him to develop a more desirable way of life in general. Presumably, more food, more leisure, and a higher level of living are automatically desirable.

Cyrus Hall McCormick invented his first primitive reaping machine in 1831. But someone was ahead of him by 1800 years or so. A Roman historian in the first century of the Christian Era, Pliny the elder, recorded the fact that "in the vast domains of the provinces of Gaul, a large hollow frame, armed with teeth and supported on two wheels, is driven through the standing wheat, the beasts being yoked behind it; the result being that the heads of the grain are torn off and fall within the frame."

McCormick's machine offered many improvements over that early Roman-French model, but the source of its power was still beasts. The efficient combine was yet many years away. Cumbersome steam threshers began to move under their own power on a few farms as early as the 1860's. And a few primitive and experimental steam tractors appeared soon afterward. But horses were to continue in the ascendency until the Twentieth Century and the coming of the lightweight and all-purpose gasoline tractor and the modern gasoline combine.

Even so, those primitive reapers (combined with John Deere's 1837 steel plow) made it possible for pioneers to settle and cultivate the vast plains of the American west. As the machines improved and increased, the amount of labor required to cultivate an acre of wheat (from plowing to delivering the wheat to the granary) steadily decreased. With the hand labor of 1830, almost 58 hours were required. With the machines of 1896, it took only nine hours. In 1940, only four hours were needed. With today's tractors, seeders, combines, trucks, and similar equipment, the job can be done in about three hours.

The present-day farmer can plow one acre in 48 minutes, against two hours and 36 minutes in 1920. Today he can dig 60 post holes in two and a half hours, versus 10 hours in 1920. A mechanical cotton picker performs the labor of more than 80 hand pickers. (It would be absurd indeed to imagine that uneconomic slave labor would have continued to be used for picking cotton if that machine had been available a hundred years ago.) Today, a mechanical green-bean picker does as much work as 50 manual pickers. As a result of using those machines, American farmers increased their production by 35 per cent between 1940 and 1955 — with no increase in acreage, and in spite of a 28 per cent decrease in farm workers!

The automobile also uses a surprising number of farm products in its construction. Among the obvious ones are cotton, wool, and hides. Among the not so obvious ones are corn, flaxseed, and soy beans. In 1956, around 2.5 million acres of farm land were needed to grow the products used by the automotive industry in the form of paints, seat coverings, and other accessories — even though the farmers were meeting increasingly heavy competition from the producers of synthetics such as nylon, orlon, rayon, and such.

Finally, according to the 1957 figures, more than one-half of all fruits and vegetables are carried by trucks to produce markets throughout the country; for frozen foods, the figure rises to 70 per cent. Around 85 per cent of all livestock goes to market in trucks. One hundred per cent of all live poultry, and 99.8 per cent of all shell eggs, move to market over the highways. Milk delivery — from farmer to city consumer — is a trucking operation. Of total farm products, about 90 per cent goes to market by motor transportation. It also works the other way around; most of the things that the farmer buys also come to him by truck.

The above summary of increased production on the farms since 1900 explains why 88 per cent of the American people can now live in urban and industrial centers instead of on farms. The figures themselves tell why farmers can afford to have television, airplanes, and vacations abroad. They also suggest why there is now little or no distinction in either appearance or income between the businessman who owns and operates a large farm and the businessman who owns and manages a fair-sized factory. The primary cause of any differences between farmers and urbanites in former times was primarily ISOLATION. And the primary reason for the abolition of those differences was the AUTOMOBILE.

Put those two words side by side. ISOLATION — AUTOMOBILE. They don't belong together. You might as well try to mix oil and water. The automobile deserves an honored place in history because — even if it had done nothing else — it permitted the farmer and his family to leave the farm whenever they felt like it and to go wherever they wished. The heart of the matter is found in the answer of a farm wife to an investigator for the United States Department of Agriculture who had asked her why they had a car but no bathtub. She replied, "Why, you can't go to town in a bathtub."

But as could have been predicted, the bathtub soon followed the car to the farm. So did the daily newspaper and the latest magazines. So did many other conveniences and necessities. For a moment, let's examine a few of the more important befores and afters.

High on the list is education. Many of the inventors of the automobile, as well as the founders of the various companies, were farm boys who had to walk two or three miles to get to the traditional little red school house and its McGuffey readers. In their reminiscences, those old timers seem always to have been walking through the snow and mud on bitter cold days. But they weren't exaggerating (at least not too much) because farm boys before 1900 only went to school during the worst months of the winter when farm work was at a minimum. When they got there, they usually found the customary one-room country school with one teacher for all classes.

The automobile changed all that. The farm boy now walks only to the road in front of his house. The school bus provides portal to portal transportation. It is probable that the average *town* pupil has to walk farther to get to school than does the

Photos Courtesy A.M.A.

Photo Courtesy A.M.A.

Photo Courtesy Chrysler Corp.

80

average farm boy!

In 1956, more than 10 million pupils travelled to school in 160,000 school buses and other vehicles regularly used for that purpose. The overwhelming majority of them were from farm and suburban areas. Those buses travelled about five million miles each school day, plus more millions of miles on those yearly student excursions to Washington and other places of historic interest. And almost 1,000 "bookmobiles" regularly brought the latest best-sellers and technical publications to millions of farm people.

The 200,000 "one-room schools" of 1916 have now decreased to around 40,000 — and the modern consolidated schools are replacing more of them every month. Even in the rural schools that still remain, most of the teachers live in town and drive to work.

It is logical to assume that any differences between city and consolidated-county schools today are determined more by the goals of the pupils than by an inherent difference in academic standards and facilities. But until the automobile came along, the country boy was at a severe educational disadvantage when compared to his city cousin.

In addition to better education for farm boys and girls, the automobile soon enabled farm wives to by-pass those sparsely-stocked crossroads stores of 1900 and to drive right on to the county seat or a large city. There she could observe the latest styles in clothing and furniture, and see those new-fangled movies or listen to a popular lecturer. The car permitted home demonstration agents from the colleges and governmental agencies to come to the farms to teach the wives the latest advances in cooking, canning, decoration, and sanitation. The refrigeration and household appliance divisions of the automobile companies also supplied the farm wife with a host of low-priced and easily-financed appliances to decrease her drudgery. That, in turn, gave her more time to enjoy the new way of life that the automobile had opened up to her.

Farm wives began to join clubs and to take a more active part in church work, P. T. A., and politics. The crossroads church with its circuit-riding minister began to disappear as the farm families joined town and city churches. Without the automobile, the life of the farm woman would necessarily have remained the drab and lonely existence it had always been — and the suicide rate among desperate, drudge-ridden, and isolated pre-automobile farm women would doubtless have continued at its customary high level.

And without the automobile, farm people in general would have continued to die unnecessarily because the doctor couldn't get there in time — or, even if he could, because he couldn't take them to a hospital.

Many doctors, in their waiting rooms, feature a picture of the old family practitioner of many years ago at the bedside of a sick child. When you look at it, you just know that (outside the picture and the house) faithful old Dobbin is waiting patiently to pull the good doctor in his buggy to another desperately ill person. Nostalgia is a wonderful thing; it helps to keep us sane and happy. But it is fortunate indeed for farm people that the automobile replaced the horse as the source of transportation for doctors.

Since the advent of the automobile, the death rate in this country has dropped by about 50 per cent. Actually, the automobile deserves almost no direct credit for that record. The big gains came from improved sanitation, immunization, drugs, and better medical knowledge in general. But indirectly, the automobile obviously played a part, especially in better medical service for the farmer.

Before the automobile, the country doctor frequently had little choice but to use the farm kitchen as his operating room. For even if there was time to get the patient to a hospital, the rough journey in a buggy or wagon was likely to prove fatal. The mortality rate from either procedure was distressingly high. But in this automobile age, we don't have country doctors any more; we have city doctors who use their automobiles to visit their patients who live on farms. A comfortable ambulance is always at hand. And a modern hospital is usually less than an hour away. The kitchen operation is now a thing of the past. Farm people receive the same medical service as city people, including mechanized pulmotors and rescue squads, traveling X-ray laboratories, mobile dental offices and health units, and so on.

It is true that another form of violent death has accompanied the advance of the automobile. While that story is reserved for the next chapter, here is an idea worthy of some consideration: If we were still faced with the pre-automobile days of crowded city living — with numerous livery stables and filthy, unpaved, horse-inhabited streets — the result might well be an increase in the death rate from diseases that would be far in excess of current automobile deaths. While that possibility in no way makes death by automobile any more desirable or excusable, it could serve to put the issue in better focus.

As mentioned earlier, farming today has become an acute political problem. And it is assumed by many farmers that their increased share of the good things of life is due primarily to governmental action. It is not here recommended that farmers give thanks to any program or person for their good fortune. By and large, they themselves have earned it by hard work and intelligent management. But if they must have a symbol to honor for their material well being, they could hardly do better than to feature the automotive industry with its cars, trucks, tractors, and refrigerators. For those things, more than anything else, were responsible for bringing farmers into the mainstream of American life.

Chapter 6

HOW TO STAY ALIVE ON THE ROADS

In 1873, the legislature of Wisconsin offered a $10,000 prize to encourage the private development of a "cheap and practical substitute for the horse" on the roads of the United States. Some 80 years later, General Motors returned the compliment by offering a $25,000 prize for a practical plan whereby the government might build better roads on which people could run their substitutes for the horse.

Two years after the Wisconsin Legislature offered that prize, it was won by a steam vehicle designed by E. P. Cowles. The practicality of his horseless carriage was proved by "racing" it against another steamer — from Madison to Green Bay and back. It took about a week to make the 200 mile trip. The delay was caused by the vehicle rather than the roads. And the legislators were so dissatisfied with the result that they gave him only half of the promised prize money.

By the time of that 1953 General Motors contest (won by the New York City Commissioner of Parks, Robert Moses), the quality of the vehicles was far superior to the quality of the roads on which they traveled. And the number of cars on them exceeded the capacity of those roads by several millions. That G-M contest was doubtless of value as a novel way of calling the problem to the attention of the American people and encouraging them to pressure our legislators into the long-overdue highway building program that is now under way.

The Federal Highway Act of 1956 is the heart of the greatest public works program in the history of the world. During the next 13 years, the government of the United States has promised to construct more roads than the Roman Empire built in 500 years. In fact, it has been estimated that this 13-year program is probably bigger than *all* the world's previous road projects combined up until the beginning of this century. This current United States road building program is more than 60 times greater than was the Panama Canal project. By 1971, more than $50 billion worth of new and improved roads may have been added to what we now have. If *all* federal, state, county, and local road building is included (both maintenance and new construction) it now seems probable that the rate of spending for roads throughout the 1960's will be more than 11 *billion* dollars yearly. Whatever else it may or may not do, that expenditure will go a long way toward bringing our highway system into harmony with the job it should be doing.

One part of the program calls for a 41,000 mile Interstate Highway System. The width will range up to eight lanes, depending on traffic needs. And the right-of-way will contain adequate space for future expansion. Those roads are to be so solidly built that parts of them may still be in use hundreds of years from now. They are being designed to accommodate the anticipated traffic needs of 1975. The Interstate Highway System will connect 48 states, 42 of the state capitals, and more than 90 per cent of all cities with a population of 50,000 or more. In length, it will measure only a little over one per cent of our total road system. But it is expected to carry more than 20 per cent of the total traffic. When it is completed, a person can drive from coast to coast and from border to border without ever encountering a traffic light. The nation will be crisscrossed by four magnificent super-highways from east to west, and eight from north to south. From an engineering viewpoint, they will be the safest highways ever built. It is estimated that they will save 3,500 lives yearly.

During its peak construction years, that new highway program will consume between five and six million tons of steel and more than 110 million barrels of cement annually. The number of direct jobs created will run between 250,000 and 300,000 — plus countless indirect jobs in the industries that will supply the machines and materials.

Who will pay for all this? You will, of course — along with

Photos Courtesy A.M.A.

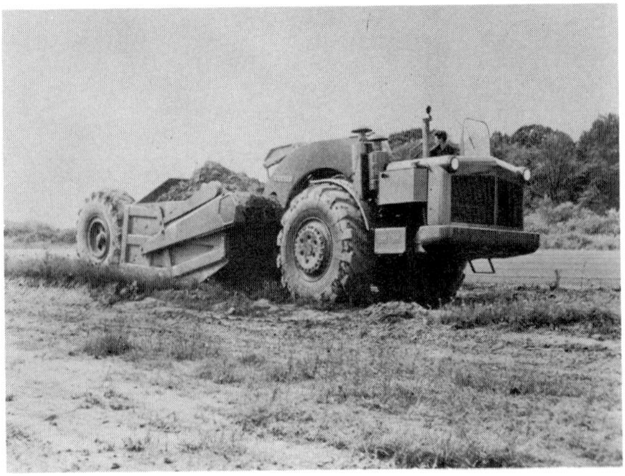

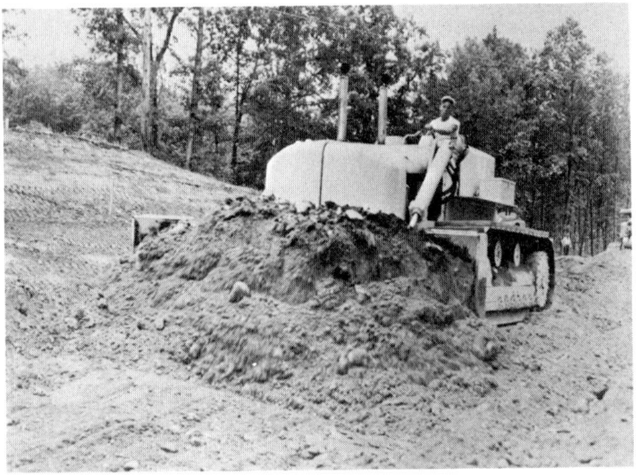

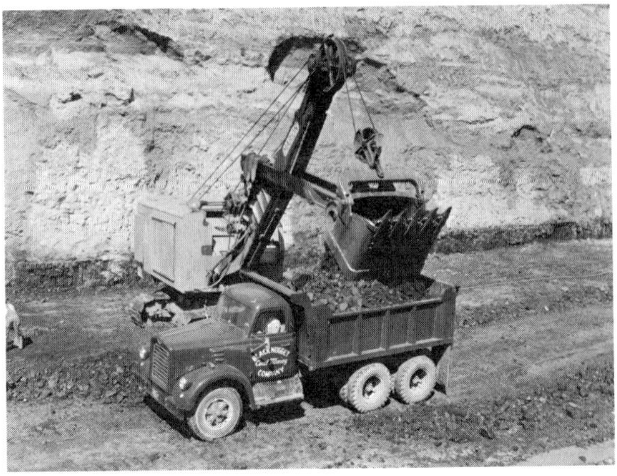

all other taxpayers. But the payment will be handled in various ways. The federal government will pay 90 per cent of the cost of the Interstate Highway System; each state will pay the remaining 10 per cent of the cost of that portion within its borders. The system will be toll free — except in a few cases where *existing* toll roads may be incorporated into the system for a limited period of time. (This program could well mean the end of the idea of paying for roads by directly charging the users.) Nor will the new roads be paid for by the sale of bonds; although a few states may use that customary method to raise their 10 per cent, the main idea is that they are to be built on a pay-as-we-go basis.

That's the announced federal highway building program, and it is now underway. But the chances of its being completed on schedule, or at the estimated cost, are so slim as to be discounted completely. (Already, at the end of 1958, the original estimates for both cost and completion date are being drastically revised — especially the cost estimates.) True enough, a government can build excellent roads, and build them fast. Adolph Hitler proved that fact conclusively when he crisscrossed Germany in a few years' time with those magnificent super highways. But, fortunately, we don't live under a dictatorship. The price we must pay for our more desirable type of government, however, is almost always delay, poor service, and high costs in those areas where the government has assumed responsibility for supplying economic goods and services. While freedom is well worth that price, perhaps more thought should be given to devising ways and means to decrease our dependence on government in this strictly economic area of producing a product and service we need, want, and are willing to pay for. Even in the complicated area of roads, the problem is fundamentally no more unsolvable than the related problems of railroads, air lines, large utilities, pipe lines, telephones, and toll roads. But since we Americans have decreed that our government must assume full responsibility for providing us with adequate roads, certainly we should at least continue to write to our state and federal congressmen and ask them to please do the best they can. It does seem a shame, however, that we must appeal to a man's patriotism and political aspirations to encourage his support for a strictly economic problem such as more and safer highways.

The automobile industry, of course, has been actively campaigning for better roads for the past 50 years. While one obvious reason for their interest is the sale of more cars, they are also acutely aware of the frightful slaughter of men, women, and children that occurs on our inadequate highways every year. The story of the Automotive Safety Foundation is one example of what the automobile industry is doing to help decrease that slaughter. The story starts in 1935, with the August issue of *The Reader's Digest.*

That issue contained one of the most effective magazine articles ever written. It was called "And Sudden Death," and the reader was advised to skip that particular article if he had a weak stomach. In vivid language, it described the gruesome results of automobile accidents, " . . . . the flopping pointless efforts of the injured to stand up; the queer, grunting noises; the steady, panting groaning of a human being with pain creeping up on him as the shock wears off . . . . the slack expression on the face of a man, drugged with shock, staring at the Z-twist in his broken leg, the insane crumpled effect of a child's body after its bones are crushed inward . . . . an hysterical woman with her screaming mouth opening a hole in the bloody drip that fills her eyes and runs off her chin . . . . the raw ends of bones protruding through flesh in compound fractures, and the dark red, oozing surfaces where clothes and skin were flayed off at once . . . . the three bodies out of one car so soaked with oil from the crankcase that they looked like wet brown cigars and not human at all; a man, walking around and babbling to himself oblivious of the dead and dying, even oblivious of the dagger-like sliver of steel that stuck out of his streaming wrist; a pretty girl with her forehead laid open, trying hopelessly to crawl out of a ditch in spite of her smashed hip." And so on and so on, with word-picture after word-picture of the fearful results produced by speed, alcohol, neglected roads, inadequate traffic laws and enforcement, emotional instability, recklessness, and just plain stupidity.

The article was effective for two reasons: First, most of the many millions of persons who read it were shocked into driving more slowly and more carefully — for awhile. But that soon wore off and the blood continued to flow. Second, and of more permanent value, the public furor that resulted from the article caused the leaders of the American automobile industry (and other industries) to wonder if there was something they could do as private citizens to slow down the annual slaughter on our highways.

But what could they do? Of course the manufacturers could build more safety features into their cars. But they had already been doing that about as fast as practical safety devices became commercially feasible. (Today, the automobile manufacturers spend almost $6 million annually on engineering research that directly results in more safety features in their cars.) Their survey of the situation, however, showed that the main trouble lay with the driver of the automobile — and the manufacturers couldn't very well control him. The next culprit was the roads — and the government had reserved that job for itself. The third cause of the slaughter was poor enforcement of laws and penalties against reckless driving — and that was also a function for which government had assumed responsibility. So since they couldn't control the driver, couldn't build good roads, and couldn't pass and enforce laws against stupid driving, just what could they do?

The final decision of the automobile manufacturers was to use their money and influence in a permanent educational campaign and research program. They hoped thereby to persuade the American people in general to do what the automobile manufacturers couldn't do themselves — to demand from their government more and better roads, better laws for safe driving, strict enforcement of the laws, and any other feasible measures that would decrease the needless slaughter of men, women, and children on our highways. At the same time, it was anticipated that the campaign would influence the people themselves to become safer drivers.

To implement their decision, the Automobile Manufacturers Association established the Automotive Safety Foundation in 1937 ". . . to promote the mutual interests of the public and the automotive industries by encouraging the safe and efficient use of streets and highways . . ."

In the beginning, the membership of the Automotive Safety Foundation (ASF) was mostly vehicle manufacturing companies. But today, it has grown to about 600 companies and associations from many different fields — automotive, oil, rubber, steel, cement, insurance, banking, advertising, and others. One-half of the budget of this non-profit organization is contributed by the members of the Automobile Manufacturers Association; the other half by interested companies and persons outside that Association. While the automobile manufacturers work extensively through their Safety Foundation, they also support various programs directly — such as AMA's 1958 grant of $150,000 to the Cornell University Crash-Injury Research Program.

In 1937 when ASF was founded, deaths from automobile accidents totaled almost 40,000; and non-fatal injuries were about 1,400,000. That was 13.3 deaths per 10,000 registered motor vehicles, and 14.7 deaths per 100 million miles driven.

In 1957, the actual number of deaths and injuries was about the same as in 1937. But deaths per 10,000 registered vehicles had decreased from 13.3 to 5.8, and deaths per 100 million miles driven had decreased from 14.7 to 5.9. Thus the death rate per mile driven has dropped by 60 per cent. The current rate versus the 1937 rate represents a 20-year saving of more

THOUSANDS OF
TRAFFIC DEATHS

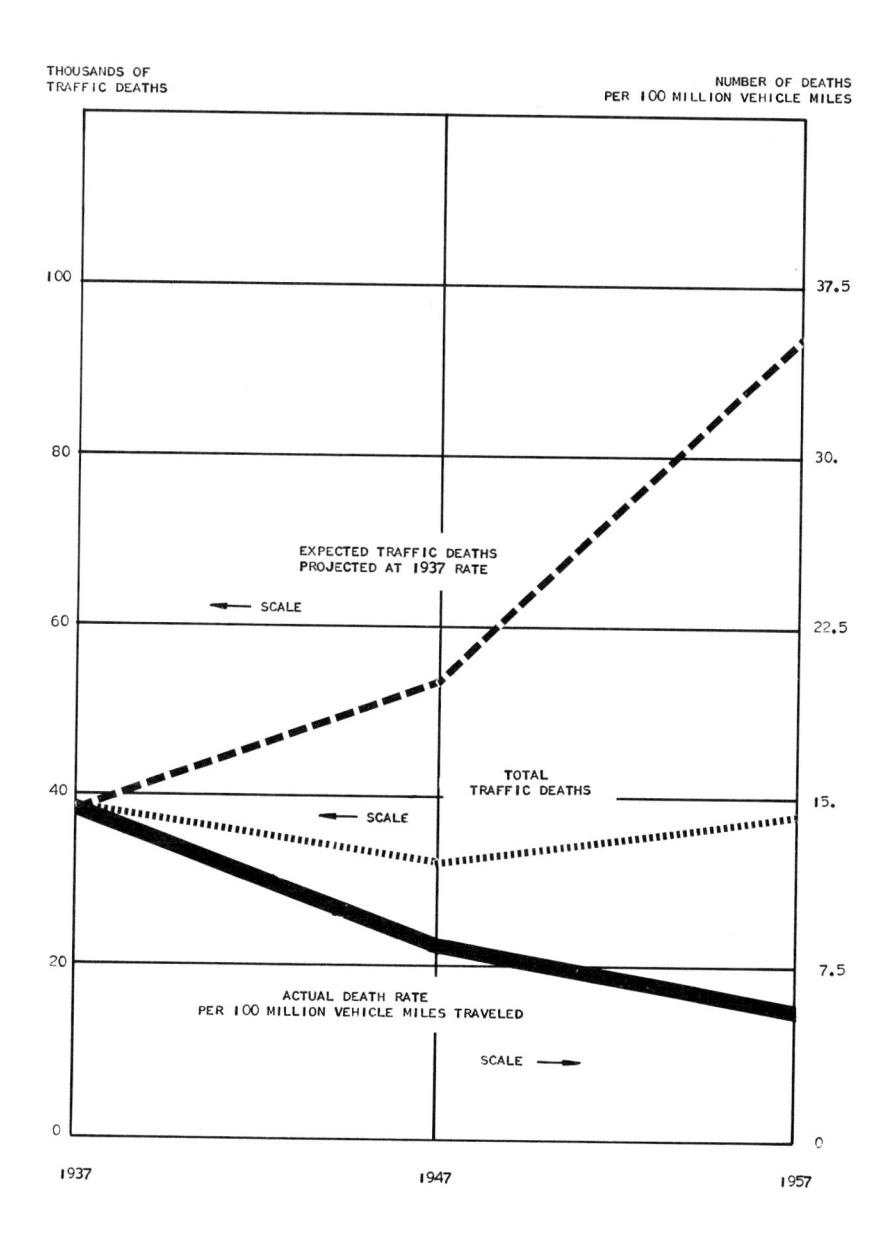

NUMBER OF DEATHS
PER 100 MILLION VEHICLE MILES

100 — 37.5

80 — 30.

EXPECTED TRAFFIC DEATHS
PROJECTED AT 1937 RATE

← SCALE

60 — 22.5

TOTAL
TRAFFIC DEATHS

40 — 15.

← SCALE

20 — 7.5

ACTUAL DEATH RATE
PER 100 MILLION VEHICLE MILES TRAVELED

SCALE →

0 — 0

1937   1947   1957

Photos Courtesy A.M.A.

than a half-million human lives, the prevention of injury to some 18 million persons, and the saving of perhaps $50 billion in lost wages, property damage, medical expense, and insurance overhead.

Obviously, that magnificent record was not due solely (or even primarily) to the efforts of the automobile industry through its Safety Foundation. Many other private organizations — especially the American Automobile Association and its state and local affiliates — have campaigned for better roads and more realistic safety laws for the past 50 years. Likewise, many governmental organizations have necessarily been involved in all these road and safety campaigns. The separate and concerted efforts of hundreds of private and governmental organizations were necessary to bring about that 60 per cent reduction in the annual rate of slaughter on our highways. But since space doesn't permit a listing of their names and accomplishments — and since this book is primarily about the automobile industry — the ASF is here offered merely as an example of the general type of work being done by all of them in the areas of safety and roads.

In 1937, only a few cities had traffic engineers. When policemen were stuck with traffic duty, they often felt somewhat like soldiers on KP. Only a handful of our schools and colleges had any courses or programs for safety education. Research facilities for traffic problems were almost nonexistent. Traffic laws varied radically from community to community and from state to state. In the few states that required a driver's license, the purpose was usually to raise revenue rather than to control unsafe drivers. And as often as not, fines for traffic violations were levied for the same purpose. In general, the politicians still followed the traditional "pork barrel" approach to highway construction — and the already-inadequate roads were steadily falling further behind the increasing use and development of automobiles.

The responsibility for the sorry situation belonged to everybody, and thus to nobody. Death ruled the road in that misty no-man's-land that is so often found between governmental ownership and private use of economic facilities in a democratic country. Politicians were elected to office by blaming the automobile manufacturers; and the manufacturers, in turn, claimed that the responsibility belonged to government. Meanwhile, the users of the manufacturers' cars and the government's roads continued to kill and maim each other by the millions. The extent of that slaughter can best be visualized from this one harsh fact: The number of killed and injured persons on our highways since 1900 exceeds by far the number of killed and injured American soldiers in all our wars combined.

When the leaders of the automobile and related industries established the Automotive Safety Foundation, they realistically faced this fact: In our form of government, the political leaders generally do whatever they think the most voters want them to do. Conversely, and by the nature of a democracy, the political leaders seldom initiate a program unless there is good evidence that the voters want it and are willing to pay the price in one form or another. (This is merely an observation on how politics works, *not* a criticism of politicians; for if they want to stay in office, they can't very well do otherwise.) Thus the number-one problem for ASF and the hundreds of other organizations interested in the same problem was to arouse and educate the American people in general to the point where they would demand better safety enforcement and better highways, and would also show a willingness to pay for them. While the details of the engineering, legal, and financial solutions to the problem were important, they were secondary to public education; for unless there was an effective public demand for them, the remedies could never be applied.

The ASF began its ever-growing and never-ending educational program by joining with 11 other similar organizations in developing the Standard Highway Safety Program For States in 1937. Later on, that idea grew into the Action Program of the President's Committee for Traffic Safety, which correlates the activities of the many organizations that are attempting in various ways to decrease the annual slaughter on our highways. At most, the automobile manufacturers deserve only a small fraction of the credit for the resulting decrease in the death rate. But, once again, the various programs participated in by their Safety Foundation will serve as a fair example of the types of work that are also being done by the others.

The Automotive Safety Foundation has participated in surveys and studies to upgrade our traffic courts, to strengthen licensing requirements, and to encourage safety teaching in our schools. (In addition, it should be noted that 8,676 cars, valued at $20.5 million, were made available during the 1957-58 school year by automobile dealers to help teach our young boys and girls how to drive better.)

ASF has helped to establish safety engineering and training centers at various universities. It also supports research projects and programs to solve the fearful problems created by traffic in our crowded cities, to reorganize outmoded local and state traffic and highway departments, and to build better and safer roads. Above all, along with hundreds of other organizations that are interested in decreasing highway accidents, the ASF attempts in every possible way to create an informed public opinion that will demand better highways and more effective safety enforcement.

Unquestionably, the various local, state, and national safety programs have produced excellent results. In a few states and communities, the job has been done so well that the death rate has been reduced to one-half of the national average. Thus it is self-evident that the annual slaughter could be immediately and drastically reduced in the high-death states and cities — if the voters demanded it and would approve a small increase in taxes to pay for the necessary safety programs *that have already been tested elsewhere and proved effective.* But considering the size and inherent difficulties of the overall problem, a remarkably superior job has still been done on a national basis.

Since almost 80 million of us fallible and emotional human beings have licenses to drive a projectile that can be as lethal as a bomb, the continuing seriousness of the problem before us cannot possibly be overstated. Better highways, safer cars, and stricter law enforcement against reckless driving will unquestionably help — especially better highways. But the most effective approach to the problem on a long-term basis would be to make it *permanently profitable,* as well as humanitarian and patriotic, for persons and organizations to work toward a decrease in the death rate on our highways. That is not now the case.

When you stop and think about it, every automobile casualty insurance company would probably go broke if a way were found to stop all automobile accidents! It so happens that the casualty insurance companies are among the leaders in devising better methods and more campaigns for safety. They are doing an excellent and selfless job. (Actually, on a short term basis, it *is* to their financial advantage to work for a decrease in highway accidents.) Even so, there is something unrealistic in an arrangement whereby a businessman is expected to work for an immediate decrease and the eventual abolition of his source of income. Apparently, there is not even one organization in our entire nation that would *directly and permanently* profit from a radical decrease in the highway accident rate. In varying degrees, that includes automobile manufacturers, repair shops, doctors, morticians, and hundreds of other businesses. If there were no automobile accidents, a hundred thousand or more of our government employees would also probably lose their jobs. But if the accident rate increases, their particular jobs will probably grow in importance and pay. Yet they, too, are expected to campaign actively for more safety devices and laws — and they do.

In theory, it may seem surprising that persons will work to decrease accidents when their immediate jobs depend on more accidents. But, consciously or subconsciously, those people are doubtless aware that, in the long run, deaths and accidents are not really profitable even to the persons who derive their current income from them. Anyway, almost no human being likes to equate a human life with a dollar bill. Even so, the harsh fact remains that the jobs and incomes of hundreds-of-thousands of persons would be enhanced by an *increase* in the highway accident rate. To some considerable extent, those are the same persons who are expected to work for safer highways!

It would be relatively simple to remove that inherent contradiction in our present arrangement by making it both profitable *and* humanitarian for almost all of those organizations and persons to devote their efforts wholeheartedly to more safety on our highways. It could be arranged so that it would become profitable to have no accidents at all, and *unprofitable* for all concerned to have even one accident. Such is now the case in coal mines, factories, railroads, department stores, and any other place where the owners and managers are subject to personal responsibility for any accident that occurs on their premises — and where the same owners and managers are subject to personal reward for keeping those accidents to a minimum. That is a wise arrangement indeed. It is almost certain that no person can resist both the humanitarian *and* the profit motives combined. In addition, it would also be far cheaper than is now the case.

Unfortunately, since nobody owns our roads, no "owner" can be held legally responsible for what happens on them. Also, the pay and promotion of the governmental managers is not directly tied to a decrease in the accident rate. The net result of that queer and uneconomic arrangement is that we users of the highways have little alternative but to battle it out among ourselves when we are involved in an accident.

The evidence is clear that almost 100 per cent of us are determined to continue that archaic and unwise system of "protecting" our lives and property on the highways. As long as that remains true, we would be well advised to give our full support to the hundreds of organizations that are now actively and effectively campaigning for more and better safety measures. And most important of all, every person owes it to himself to drive more carefully. Under any circumstances, that is the first step toward a solution to this acute problem of highway safety.

Chapter 7
THE LAST BILLIONAIRE

A man named Albert Strelow once passed up a large fortune because he thought the profits of Ford Motor Company were too small.

Strelow was a hard-working carpenter who had established a successful paint and carpenter business in Detroit around 1900. In 1903, he reconditioned an old wagon shop he owned, and rented it out for $75 a month to the newly-formed Ford Motor Company as its first headquarters and factory.

The founders of that company had lots of ideas and plans, but not much cash. So they offered their landlord a five per cent interest in the company for $5,000. He took it.

The new company was successful from the start. Strelow got more than $15,000 in dividends over the next four years, plus an exceptionally high increase in the value of his stock. Then he heard about a promising gold mine in Canada. So he sold his 50 shares of Ford stock for $25,000 — and bought into the gold mining venture. As sometimes happens, the mining venture proved to be more glitter than gold, and Strelow lost his money. Some years later, he applied to the Ford Motor Company for a job.

If he had held on to his stock for another 12 years until Henry Ford bought out his minority stockholders, he would have received a total return on his $5,000 investment of about $18 million.

A Detroit school teacher risked her savings of $100 in the new venture in 1903. When she sold her single share in 1919, she had received a total return of $355,000 on her investment.

A young clerk invested $1,000 in cash — plus a note for an additional $1,400 — and went to work for the new company. He used a small part of his dividends to pay off his note and to buy a few more shares of stock. After 16 years, he sold his stock for $30 million.

Nobody really knows how much Henry Ford himself got. At one time, he was offered a billion dollars for his company. By then, he had drawn many millions in dividends and salary, and had extensive other holdings.

Can the effort and contribution of any one man really be worth a billion dollars to his fellow men? This writer casually put that question to 29 of his friends, associates, and acquaintances. All of them are college graduates. All of them hold executive positions in various companies. The question was put to them in such a way that they had no idea they were being interviewed. In different ways and in different words, each of the 29 replied that no man could possibly be worth a billion dollars to his fellow men. Admittedly, 29 is a small sample, but it is here assumed that the result of the test generally represents the viewpoint of most business leaders in America today. Perhaps their viewpoint is the correct one. Perhaps it isn't. At any rate, the career of Henry Ford should be examined before a final decision is made. Just how did he manage to gain control of a billion dollars and more? Did he really earn it?

Henry Ford had already been in two unsuccessful automobile manufacturing ventures before 1903 and the founding of the Ford Motor Company. In none of the three ventures did he put up any actual cash. In each instance, he swapped his mechanical know-how and improved motor for an interest in the company — always a minority interest — and went to work for the company on a salary basis.

In the third and successful venture, Henry Ford and most of his partners were soon in strong disagreement on company policy. Ford wanted to use almost all of the company's earnings for expansion. Most of the other stockholders favored a more even split between expansion and dividends.

But most controversial of all was Henry Ford's obsession with the idea that he could make a good car for $500 that would be bought by millions of Americans! That's what he wanted the company to do. But in the early 1900's, Ford's vision of a mass-produced and low-priced car to put an entire nation on wheels seemed like a crazy idea to his partners and stockholders.

The controversy continued. So Ford decided that the best solution to the problem was to gain control of the company for himself. And that's what he did.

Alexander Malcomson, the man who was Henry Ford's equal partner in establishing the company, sold his 255 shares to Ford for $175,000. That was about seven times their original value. That purchase — added to his own original 255 shares — made Ford the majority stockholder in the 1,000-share company. Thus, in 1906, he became his own boss, and thereafter did mostly as he pleased.

In 1919, after a suit by the minority stockholders compelled him to pay bigger dividends, Ford decided to buy out the remaining stockholders and become sole owner of the company. He did, and the company became a totally family-owned enterprise.

There may have been no Ford Motor Company without the original financial backing of Malcomson. That is a debatable proposition. But this much is certain: There would have been no Ford Motor Company — and no Model T — without Henry Ford.

This study is not intended to deny in any way the vital contributions of men like Edsel Ford, John and Horace Dodge, James Couzens, Walter Flanders, Norval Hawkins, Peter Martin, Harold Wills, Charles Sorensen, William Knudsen, and the many others who devoted their genius to the success of the Ford Motor Company. Henry Ford could not have done it without their help. But while acknowledging the vital part played by Ford's partners and employees, this chapter is primarily the story of Henry Ford himself. Was *his* contribution to the American people worth the billion dollars he got from them in profits? Just what did he do for that money?

Some of Ford's critics claim that Henry Ford himself contributed few, if any, truly new and original ideas to the development of the automobile. For example, they point out that Ford once defeated a patent infringement suit against his company by proving that his automobile engine was basically the same engine that had been invented in France in 1860 by Jean Lenoir.

Who deserves the credit for the mass production and efficiency concept of an assembly arrangement that brought the work to the man, instead of the other way around? At the Ford Motor Company, that idea was developed into an art that astounded everyone who saw it. But as Ford himself wrote, "The idea [for a moving assembly line] came in a general way from the overhead trolley that the Chicago packers use in dressing beef." Actually, the basic idea had been used successfully more than a century before either the meat packers or Ford Motor Company adapted it to their particular needs. In fact, the original idea may well have been conceived by the Venetian shipbuilders who were "mass producing" boats in the Thirteenth Century.

Ford's policy of taking a small profit on many units, instead of a large profit on a few units, had been profitably used by many producers in other lines long before Henry Ford began producing his Model T. And several of those earlier manufacturers were also aware that it's good business to service the product you manufacture and sell.

Specialization, division of labor, and interchangeable parts were standard practices among American gun makers long before Henry Ford was born. (The builders of the great cathedrals in Europe during the Eleventh Century were also familiar with those ideas.) And the first manufacturer who ever had trouble with a supplier of raw materials or parts was well aware that vertical integration — Ford's program to own or control his sources of supply — may be profitable from several different viewpoints.

According to Mr. Ford himself, he gained his success by basing his actions on these five ideas and principles:
1. He observed that the American people could use millions of cars.
2. It was obvious to him that a durable and inexpensive *single* model was necessary to meet that need and demand.
3. He decided that the needed millions of vehicles could be produced both cheaply and profitably by weaving together both new and old technological elements into an industrial complex designed to mass produce the type of car he had in mind.
4. His actual experience soon confirmed his belief that price reduction would result in market expansion.
5. He was of the opinion that high wages would mean more customers and, as a result, more profits.

Whether or not Henry Ford contributed new ideas, or merely improved upon existing ideas, is not at all vital to this story. The important question is this: Why was he so much more successful than his early competitors who had full access to the same ideas and inventions?

Well, there were two primary reasons. First, he and his associates applied and perfected all the above ideas (and many more) better than had ever been done before. Second, Henry Ford had a vision that drove him on. He actually *wanted* the American farmers and factory workers to own and drive their own cars. He dreamed of a world in which everyone would be prosperous and happy. As he said, he put service first and the profits just naturally followed.

It can't be proved, but perhaps Ford's vision was a more powerful incentive than his profits. At any rate, he often claimed it was. We are safe in assuming that if either the profits or the vision had faltered in the beginning, there would have been no Ford Motor Company as we know it today.

Let's examine that vision — Henry Ford's "crazy idea" that he could build a car so cheap and so good that millions of people would buy one. When he first talked about it, most of his listeners tended to dismiss him as a crackpot. But as we know, Mr. Ford stayed with his idea. And his famous Model T made its appearance late in 1908.

In the beginning, the price was not $500 but $825. But even so, as the advertisements said with some justice, "No car over $2,000 offers more except in trimmings."

True enough, there were no trimmings — and the car wasn't exactly beautiful to gaze upon. But it was simple to operate and repair, and it generally got you where you wanted to go. If there happened to be a good road handy, the Model T would operate just fine on it. But its specialty was rough roads, mud holes, ruts, and bridgeless streams — just the sort of practical and rugged vehicle demanded by the road conditions of that time. And Henry Ford was right — the people began buying them by the thousands, then by the hundreds-of-thousands, and finally by the millions.

In 1909, the Ford Motor Company produced and sold 10,607 cars. That was less than 10 per cent of the total number of cars produced and sold by the entire automobile industry that year.

By 1914, Ford had 42 per cent of the total business with 248,307 Model T's. Meanwhile, his price had dropped to $440, with a promise to refund $50 of that price to all purchasers during 1915 if the company sold 300,000 cars during the year.

That goal was easily exceeded and the refunds promptly made. Anyone could buy a car for $390. And old but still serviceable Model T's could be had for less than $100. Henry Ford's crazy idea of a mass-produced and low-priced automobile was no longer considered crazy. His concept of an America on wheels was well on its way to reality.

It was also in 1914 that Mr. Ford initiated his revolutionary policy of a minimum wage of $5 for an eight-hour working day.

The automobile workers had always earned a higher wage than their counterparts in other industries. If they hadn't, they would never have left their old jobs in the first place — espe-

Henry Ford in His First Car

Model T

Photos Courtesy Ford Motor Co.

1903—1959

In the Beginning

Photos Courtesy Ford Motor Co.

Now

108

cially not the trained mechanics that the new industry had to have. But Ford's $5 minimum was more than double the going rate!

The automobile workers had also generally worked shorter hours than employees in the older industries. But Ford's policy was an eight-hour day at a time when twelve hours was still the standard in many places.

The announcement of that revolutionary labor policy of Ford Motor Company caused a riot in Detroit. More than 10,000 men actually stormed the plant in their frenzy to get jobs.

Also in 1914, the profits of the Ford Motor Company exceeded $30 million. Most of that belonged to Mr. Ford himself, and as majority stockholder he controlled the disposition of all of it.

Here is what Henry Ford gave in return for that multi-million-dollar profit. He produced an excellent car for $390. He paid wages twice as high as his competitors. He cut the working day down to eight hours.

In 1921, a depression year, Ford produced and sold 845,000 Model T's. That was almost 55 per cent of the total passenger automobile business. It was, of course, a better car than the one of 1914. The price was also lower — $325. And the Ford employees were earning higher wages. Henry Ford's *personal profit* for the year was about $75 million.

In 1923, Ford produced more than two million cars and trucks. Every few seconds, a new Model T rolled off the end of that world-famous assembly line. But even so, Ford sales dropped to less than half of the total automobile business for that year.

In 1925, the Ford Motor Company sold about 1.5 million cars — and its percentage of the total sales for the industry dropped closer to 40 per cent. In 1926, Ford's percentage of the business dropped to about 33 per cent, and the outlook was for a continued steady decline.

On May 26, 1927, Henry Ford produced his last Model T.

After making 15 million of them, he stopped production and closed down his plants. Why?

The answer is simplicity itself. The American people had stopped buying them! They bought some, of course, but not as they used to. They were buying cars made by Ford's competitors — Chevrolet, Overland, Dodge, Essex.

In an effort to hold his market in the mid-1920's, Henry Ford chanted his magic formula once again. Raise wages, he said. And increase production, improve the product, and cut prices. It was done. For a short while during that period, the Model T "Runabout" was priced at $260.

That tried and true formula had always worked before. It had always brought *more* sales and *more* profits, not less. It had made Henry Ford a billionaire. But this time, it didn't work. After 1924, sales and profits continued downward. The consumers preferred to pay a higher price for a Chevrolet. Ford's declining profits soon turned into heavy losses. What had happened?

In the early 1920's, Ford's competitors had decided that the American people were willing to pay a higher price for a more stylish car, a closed car, a more comfortable car, a car with a gear shift and similar mechanical improvements. Mr. Ford disagreed, and stayed with his rough-and-ready Model T.

He was wrong and his competitors were right. The consumers said so, with their own money — and Henry Ford's Model T was through. Later on, he came back with his Model A, but that is another story. (Ironically, the vast changes brought about by the Model T seem to have made the instrument of the change itself obsolescent!)

True enough, no one man was responsible for putting America on wheels and for perfecting machines that enabled farmers all over the world to produce more in less time and with less toil. And no single person, however dedicated, deserves more than a fraction of the credit for creating completely new industries and changing the living and thinking habits of the people of an entire nation. It required the full time and best efforts of many men to supply the tools and know-how that enabled millions of workers to earn more by producing more, and thus to lead more comfortable and happier lives. But, unquestionably, Henry Ford was the leader of the few thousands who do deserve the credit for it.

Was Ford's leadership and contribution worth the billion dollars and more that he got in profits? Or did Henry Ford profit at the expense and loss of his customers and the American people in general?

Well, first, he didn't force anyone to buy his product. He couldn't. Millions of free and independent persons voluntarily chose to exchange their hard-earned money for a Model T, rather than to buy something else with it. In fact, they sometimes put their names on a list and waited many months for delivery.

Those purchasers of Model T's were of the strong opinion that they profited by the exchange. That's the only reason they bought them. And when they no longer considered the Model T a good buy, they bought the product offered by Ford's competitors.

Beyond any question, the employees of Ford Motor Company were sure that they profited by swapping their labor for Ford wages. There were hundreds of eager applicants for every available job.

Ford's dealers, agents, and sub-contractors profited greatly from their business with him. There was much competition for those Model T agencies. And many of the dealers became millionaires in their own right.

The Ford Motor Company was naturally one of the nation's largest taxpayers, as well as the source of the earnings of hundreds-of-thousands of other taxpayers. So the government certainly profited in many ways — including war production — from Ford's efforts.

From a social viewpoint, Henry Ford was a pioneer in hiring

Negroes, physically handicapped persons, and old people who wanted to work but couldn't get jobs elsewhere. He also hired hundreds of probationary ex-convicts who otherwise would have been kept in prison. Certainly they profited. The American people in general also profited greatly when Henry Ford fought and defeated the "Selden patent" that once threatened to monopolize and hamstring the young automobile industry. The living and working conditions of industrial employees throughout the country (and in various foreign nations as well) were improved immeasurably when Mr. Ford gave the architect, Albert Kahn, free rein to express his revolutionary ideas about changing the dark and dismal factories of the early 1900's into the bright, clean, and airy places that are now the general rule. And we should never forget that Henry Ford offered a *new* car at the lowest price the world has ever known — $260.

By any meaningful and realistic test, Henry Ford earned every penny of his vast fortune. It was rightfully his to do with as he chose. It so happens that he chose to establish the Ford Foundation to give most of it away for the purpose of hospitals, education, and other similar projects for the general public.

We American people have now arranged our government and economy so that there can never again be another billionaire. In a democracy, we have the political right to do that if we want to. But that fact has no bearing whatever on whether or not the services of a person may be worth a billion dollars to his fellow men.

Chapter 8
HOW TO GET TO THE TOP

The gasoline automobile was largely invented by Europeans, mostly French and German. The Daimler Motor Company of Germany was producing cars for export before 1890. By the time the Duryea brothers built their first automobile in the United States in 1893, gasoline cars were racing all over the excellent highways of France. That first Duryea car ran, but it didn't run far. It is preserved in the Smithsonian Institute — in a somewhat modified and rebuilt form. Mechanically, it was vastly inferior to its European predecessors. And anyway, the poor roads in the United States at that time would soon have shaken it to pieces.

At the time the Duryea brothers were wondering if their "horseless carriage" would even run, the Parisian automobile firm of Panhard-Levassor was actually selling its remarkably modern cars from an illustrated catalogue. Eight years or so were to pass before the United States could boast of such an accomplishment. Even so, after the turn of the century, the automobile soon became commonplace in the land of its adoption, while it remained a mere plaything of the rich in the lands of its birth. Why?

Many answers have been offered to explain that fact, such as the greater need for transportation in the United States, the technical skills found among our people, our greater purchasing power, our compelling desire to keep up with our neighbors in material possessions, a favorable political climate, and so on. Each of those reasons is valid, especially the one concerning political climate. But within that setting of a favorable political climate, perhaps the biggest reason of all has been largely overlooked — the American's desire to get to the top or to become his own boss.

At the beginning of this century, anyone could go into the

automobile business if he had a few thousand dollars — or if he had mechanical ability and could find someone to finance him. For example, as we have already noted, Henry Ford never originally invested a penny in the three automobile companies with which he was associated. And the total "paid in" capital of Ford Motor Company in 1903 was only $28,000. Thousands of persons became part or sole owners of automobile companies with an original investment of little more than the proverbial shoestring.

There was absolutely no barrier against entry into the field because of race or religion. A man with a yellow or black skin was just as privileged to begin producing automobiles as was the man with the white skin. A Moslem had the same opportunity as the Christian and Jew. The immigrant was on an equal footing with the native born. Patent applications for new inventions didn't ask about the race or religion of the inventor. In short, the business of building and selling automobiles was open to anyone who wished to try; no quarter was asked, and certainly none was given.

The new industry offered full opportunity for the traditional American dream of getting rich quick or becoming one's own boss. From 1900 to 1925, more than 1,400 automobile companies were formed by thousands of people. The overwhelming majority of those early automobile producers came from poor or middle class families. Only a handful were wealthy when they started. And in proportion, those with money failed just as fast as those without. The financial background of the producer was unimportant; if a person had the ability to produce, manage, and sell, he got to the top in a hurry. The automobile industry was an example of that American dream at its best. It still is.

Some people will scoff at that statement. Included among the scoffers will be a considerable number of impatient or frustrated persons on all levels of management. They will claim that while the average man may have full opportunity in textbook theory, he doesn't have much of a chance in actual practice.

Well, let's see — by beginning first with General Motors, a widely-owned stock corporation, and briefly examining the backgrounds of its presidents.

The surest way to get to the top in a hurry is, of course, to organize your own company. Then you can start at the top. That's what William C. Durant did back in 1908 when he organized General Motors Corporation.

True enough, Durant came from an old Massachusetts-Michigan family that was certainly financially comfortable, but that fact played no part whatever in his career in the transportation business. He entered it by manufacturing road carts. In 1885, he bought the patent rights to a two-wheeled "improved suspension" cart for $1,500 — and gave up his successful insurance agency to devote full time to his new interest. He went into business with another young man, Josiah Dallas Dort, a hardware clerk, in Flint, Michigan, who put up $1,000 for a half interest in the venture. Since they had no plant of their own, the partners originally contracted with various other companies to make the carts for them at $8 each. Then they sold them for $12.50 each, a surprisingly low price for such a cart. The two young men soon owned their own carriage company, and their production of the road carts rapidly increased to 50,000 yearly. Before he was 40, Durant was a millionaire.

When the new and foundering Buick Motor Company was looking for additional capital in 1904, the owners approached Durant. Even though the company had produced only 16 cars the previous year, Durant was most interested. In October of 1904, he became chief executive officer of the reorganized and greatly expanded company. In 1908, Buick manufactured 8,487 cars in the largest automobile plant in the world. That was the year Durant established General Motors by completing a merger of Buick, Oldsmobile, and Oakland — three of the largest companies and most respected automobile names in the industry. Within the next two years, "the world's best salesman and greatest promoter" added 17 more companies to General Motors. But he overreached himself in the process.

In 1910, General Motors was threatened with receivership as a bankrupt company. Two eastern bankers finally agreed to supply the capital needed to prevent receivership, if Mr. Durant would resign. He did — but as we shall see, he was soon to return. Meanwhile, the bankers successfully operated General Motors under "interim control" while they searched for a new chief executive. They finally selected Charles W. Nash in 1912.*

It is doubtful that even Horatio Alger could have visualized such a rugged path to the top as the one followed by Charles Nash. When he was six years old, his parents separated, and their young son was "bound out" to a Michigan farmer as a chore boy. In return for his services until he reached the age of 21, the farmer was to feed him, clothe him, provide him a place to sleep, and permit him to go to school for three months each winter — if young Charles cared to walk two miles through the snow to get to school. (He did.) On his 21st birthday, Nash was to receive three suits of clothes and $100 in cash from his employer.

The terms of the arrangement were not quite as bad as they may sound. In effect, the farmer was expected to treat the boy pretty much as one of his own children. There is no evidence to indicate that young Charles was treated unjustly or more harshly than other farm boys in the 1870's. Even so, when he was 12 years old, he ran away. In a neighboring community, he found a job as an apprentice to a farmer who was also a part-time carpenter. It was a room and board arrangement, plus a little actual cash. Over the years, young Nash developed into a

---

*Technically speaking, Durant was not president of the company he founded and directed. He assigned the title to two other men during 1908-1910. And when the bankers assumed control, they also assigned the job temporarily to two more men during 1910-1912 while they were looking for a man to fill the job permanently. Thus, because of the merely nominal nature of the title during that period, those four men are not here discussed. But even if they were, it would not materially change the story.

respected and successful carpenter and farm manager.

At the age of 28, Charles Nash left the farm and moved to town. Eventually he found a job at $1.25 a day as a trimmer for the Flint Road Cart Company. In three months, he became superintendent of 150 men. That cart company became the Durant-Dort Carriage Company. As we know, one of the owners of that carriage company organized General Motors in 1908. William C. Durant thought highly enough of the work of Nash to recommend him for the presidency of the Buick Motor Company — the keystone of G-M — in 1910. Nash's superior job of reorganizing and expanding that company caused him to be elected to the presidency of General Motors itself in 1912. Later on, he left General Motors to assume control of the Thomas B. Jeffery Company, which soon became the Nash Motor Company. (Today it's the American Motors Corporation.)

When William Durant stepped down as top man in General Motors, he didn't depart from the automobile business. He organized the Chevrolet Motor Company in New Jersey in 1911. The rise of Chevrolet under Durant's direction was both fast and profitable.

Throughout this period, Durant was planning and working to regain control of General Motors. He knew he couldn't do it by himself. So he persuaded his Delaware neighbor, the E. I. du Pont de Nemours Company (and family), to enter the automobile business with him. By September of 1915, the Durant-du Pont combination (plus their friends, business associates, families, and the Chevrolet Motor Company) had purchased enough General Motors stock to give them working control of the corporation. The next year, General Motors had a new president — William C. Durant.

When Durant was again in control of the company he had founded, he plunged back into the expansionist policy that had brought him to grief in 1910. During the war years, his policy worked well. But during the 1920 depression, General Motors once more found itself in an over-extended position. The price of its stock began a rapid decline on the market. In an effort to halt it, Durant himself began buying every share that was offered for $20 or less. In short order, he had committed himself to more than $35 million — and the stock was still falling.

Aside from Durant's personal speculation, General Motors itself was also in a shaky financial position. It needed an $80 million loan to permit it to consolidate its over-extended plant and inventory. One condition of the necessary bank loan to G-M in 1920 was that the corporation be reorganized under a new president. So once again, William C. Durant was forced to resign. As he had done on the previous occasion, Durant attempted a comeback with another automobile company — Durant Motors. His announced objective was to expand it into a rival of General Motors. But the magic touch was gone; Durant Motors was a costly failure. In 1936, Durant filed a personal bankruptcy petition in which he listed his total liabilities at $914,000 and his total assets at $250. The founder and two-time chief of General Motors ended up as the working proprietor of a bowling alley. But to the last, he remained expansionist in his outlook; when he died in 1947, he was talking about a plan to expand his bowling alley into a national chain.

At the bankers' suggestion, a man with extensive corporate business experience, Pierre S. du Pont, was elected president of General Motors in the 1920 reorganization. Even with him at the helm, the company still lost $38 million in 1921 — but that's the last time it ever suffered a loss on a total year's operations.

Thus the background of the first three operating presidents of General Motors: Durant, flamboyant promoter; Nash, farm boy who made good; du Pont, business-trained scion of one of the richest industrial families in America. In 1923, the vice president in charge of operations, Alfred P. Sloan, Jr. succeeded to the presidency. At the time, Mr. du Pont said of him: "The greater part of the successful development of the corporation's operations — and the building up of a strong manufacturing and sales organization — is due to Mr. Sloan."

Alfred Sloan was graduated from the Massachusetts Institute of Technology in 1895. Soon thereafter, he went to work for the Hyatt Roller Bearing Company as an engineer and salesman. He was president of the company in 1916 when it was merged with four other accessory and parts companies into United Motors Corporation. He was also president of that combination in 1918 when the Durant expansion program brought it into General Motors. Thus Mr. Sloan's entire career was in the automobile business. He came from "a family background of learning and culture but in no sense of wealth."

The next president of General Motors, William S. Knudsen, was an immigrant who had been a bicycle mechanic in Denmark. When he arrived in America, he was not, as has so often been reported, penniless; he had $35. And he immediately set out to see if he could add something to it. For three years, he worked at various odd jobs of a mechanical nature. At age 23, he got a job as a mechanic with the John R. Keim Mills in Buffalo, a factory that made metal parts for various automobile companies — mostly Ford. When Ford Motor Company bought the Keim Mills, they automatically got Knudsen. He worked his way to the top echelon in that company by establishing Ford assembly plants all over the country. In 1922, he was hired by Mr. Sloan to manage the Chevrolet Division of General Motors. When Alfred Sloan became chairman of the board in 1937, Mr. Knudsen succeeded him as president.

Thus the first five operating presidents of General Motors: Durant and Sloan, from "financially comfortable" backgrounds; du Pont, rich family; Nash and Knudsen, apprentice carpenter and immigrant mechanic.

In 1941, another engineer became president of G-M, Charles E. Wilson. His school-teacher parents were neither rich nor poor. When Wilson was graduated from Carnegie Tech in 1909, he went to work for Westinghouse as an electrical engineer. In 1919, he was hired by General Motors to be chief engineer and factory manager of its Delco-Remy electrical division. Over the years, he held successively more important jobs in various divisions of G-M. When the directors of General Motors were looking for a successor to Knudsen, they decided that engineer Wilson was the best man available to direct the operations of the corporation under the prevailing circumstances.

The successor to Wilson, Harlow H. Curtice, answered the following classified ad in *The Flint Journal* of April 23, 1914: "WANTED — a high grade young man for office position requiring some bookkeeping experience. A fine opportunity for the right applicant." Since 20-year-old Harlow Curtice had recently studied accounting at Ferris Institute, he got the job as a bookkeeper for The AC Spark Plug Company, a subsidiary of General Motors. After holding successively more important jobs in that spark plug company, and then in the Buick Division of G-M, Mr. Curtice was elected president of General Motors in 1953.

When Harlow Curtice retired in 1958, the title of chief executive officer of General Motors was vested in a new chairman of the board, Frederic G. Donner. At the same time, an engineer, John F. Gordon, became president and chief operating officer. Chairman Donner rose to the top job in G-M along the financial route. After graduating in 1923 from the University of Michigan (Phi Beta Kappa), he spent the next three years with a Chicago accounting firm. He was hired by General Motors in 1926. At age 38, Mr. Donner was elected vice president of G-M in charge of its financial staff. The new president of General Motors, John Gordon, was graduated from the Naval Academy in 1922, and then went on to the University of Michigan for a master's degree in mechanical engineering. He started with G-M in 1923 as a laboratory assistant at 60 cents an hour. Both of those men came from family backgrounds that were exceedingly modest from a financial viewpoint.

There we have the briefest possible biographies of the eight

1912 Chevrolet

1959 Chevrolet

1903 Buick

1959 Buick

121

1904 Olds

1959 Olds

1902 Cadillac

1959 Cadillac

operating presidents of General Motors Corporation. One was born rich. Five were born into middle class families, ranging from low to upper. Two were from poor families. In view of that record (not untypical of American industry in general), it is difficult to understand how any reasonable person could give even passing consideration to the idea that only the privileged few can get to the top in industrial America; that the "average man" doesn't have much chance in an economy where the productive facilities and resources are privately owned.

All eight of those men got to the top because the Board of Directors (who had been elected by the stockholders) thought that each one was the best possible man available at the time to manage the destiny of General Motors. And when the time comes for those directors to select still another president for G-M, they will give primary consideration to these two qualifications: First, he must understand the automobile business as well as, or better than, any other available person. Second, he must have superior knowledge of General Motors and its particular problems. Thus it is practically certain that the next president of G-M is already an employee of the corporation.

There are also other requirements — personality, fundamental knowledge of economics and politics, general appearance, speaking ability, public service record, respect for and from other people, and so on through a long list of specifics and intangibles. The amount of stock owned by the candidate will not influence the judges one way or the other. While the winning candidate obviously can't be a man without friends, he most definitely won't be chosen because of personal friendships. In short, the winner will be selected by the Board of Directors solely because, all things considered, they think he is the man most likely to insure the continued success and prosperity of General Motors.

But how about the family owned or controlled company? Is ability also the determining factor there? Well, as merely one of many possible examples, let's again look briefly at the family-owned Ford Motor Company.

It is generally conceded (this writer has found *no* exception) that Henry Ford's only son, Edsel, was one of the top automobile men of his time. He began working in his father's factory as soon as he was big enough to paste stamps on envelopes. Over the years, he did all sorts of jobs in the company. From the beginning, he was specifically trained to become president of the extensive Ford operations. And in due course, he was appointed to that position. Since he died while his father was still active in the company, we can never know just what he might have done if the entire responsibility had been his. But if Edsel Ford had been in the market for a new job, there is no question but that several large automobile companies would have been most pleased to hire him as chief executive officer.

The grandson, Henry Ford II, is now president of Ford Motor Company. The evidence is clear that he was and is the man for the job. After he became chief executive officer, both the competitive and profit positions of the company improved markedly. That is the best possible test of a person's ability to run a business. If both the competitive and the profit positions of the company were to begin a steady decline together, you may rest assured that someone else would eventually be running the company. That is just as true for a family corporation as for a general stockholders corporation, *possibly even more so*, because the family controlled corporations can usually move faster. If they fail to move in time, the result is both sure and simple — like any other company in a competitive economy, they go bankrupt.

One of young Henry Ford's first actions when he assumed responsibility for the direction of Ford Motor Company in 1946, was to bring in the best talent he could find to help him run the business. The top jobs (for example, chairman of the board) are as open to the man named John Doe or Ernest Breech as they are to the grandsons named Ford. Ability is just as welcome (and just as highly rewarded) in a family corporation like Ford as it is in a general ownership corporation like G-M.

Finally, the 1985 president-to-be of General Motors (or of United States Steel or any other widely-owned industrial corporation) is probably one of the young men among that batch of business and engineering graduates that the company hired more or less routinely last June. No one could possibly pick him out at this time. But in due course, he will begin to show his superiors that he is capable of holding a top job in the company. When he does, he'll get it. In a free society and competitive economy, it's just that simple.

Chapter 9
HOW MUCH IS AN EXECUTIVE WORTH?

A favorite newspaper feature is the yearly "best" list of such things as best dressed women, all-star baseball and football teams, most important politicians, and so on. One such annual list that arouses much interest is the names and salaries of the men and women who earned $100,000 or more during the year.

While the president of a steel company led the list for 1957, a dozen or so top executives from the automobile industry were, as usual, among the runners-up. The list also included the customary sprinkling of personalities from the entertainment world — sports, movies, stage, radio and television.

Both the highly paid entertainers and the high salaried business executives are, of course, subject to the same high tax rate on their incomes. But the spontaneous reaction of the general public toward the tax payments of those two groups seems quite different. There is little doubt that the sad plight of the highly taxed entertainers often tends to arouse our sympathy. That general reaction is pin-pointed most clearly in the case of the popular and appealing winners on television quiz shows. Most of us seem instinctively to wish that there were some way they could keep more of their winnings.

The general public seldom reacts in the same way toward the business executive and his equally enormous tax payments. The distinction can, of course, be partly explained by the American tradition of admiration and good wishes for "little people" who suddenly make good. But a more basic reason for the distinction may be somewhat as follows: We are well aware that the top people in the entertainment world have real talent. We know for sure that Perry Como can sing better than we can, and that Helen Hayes is a superior actress. We know that influence and pull have no particular bearing on their popularity. If we could sing as well as Patti Page — or act as well as Jack

Benny — we are confident that we, too, would soon be earning those top salaries. We do not begrudge the high salaries that are paid to baseball players like Ted Williams and Stan Musial because we have no doubt that they earn them. And we know further that if we could hit a baseball better than they can, we would soon have similar jobs at still higher pay.

But those top salaried businessmen — well, somehow, that's different. We ourselves work hard in the same commercial world with those executives, and we can't seem to break into that magic top circle. So, since our own abilities aren't recognized as fast as we think they should be, perhaps ability really hasn't too much to do with it after all. In fact, many of us are probably reasonably sure that we could do just as good a job as our bosses — who seem mostly to perform merely the function of delegating the real work on down the line to us underlings.

That hazy concept of the purpose and function of the highly paid business leader is involved in all employee-employer relationships — in the automobile industry and elsewhere. Since those relationships are vital to our society, it might be of some value to try to find out just what services those executives do perform in return for their large salaries. And since, for many years, Walter P. Chrysler of automobile fame was paid more than a million dollars a year, let's start with him. Who paid him 300 or 400 dollars an hour — and for doing what?

Chrysler was an especially prominent member of that legendary "rags to riches" group that is encountered so frequently in the automotive industry. In many ways, his career was a close parallel to that of the fabulous Henry Ford himself. Kansas was still a frontier state when Walter Chrysler was born there in 1875. During his childhood, Indian raiders were still scalping an occasional settler in the isolated sections of that state.

While young Walter was completing the sparse schooling available in his small town of Ellis, he ran a milk route for his mother, sold calling cards, worked as a delivery boy and swept floors for the railroad. At the age of 18, he was hired as an apprentice machinist by Union Pacific at 5 cents an hour — bring your own tools. After more than three years as an apprentice with that railroad, he quit his 15 cents an hour job and went with Santa Fe as a journeyman mechanic at the top pay of 27 cents an hour. Several years (and several railroads) later, he had worked himself up to master mechanic with the Colorado and Southern at $115 a month. At age 30, he was earning $140 a month as foreman of two divisions of that railroad. A year later (with still another railroad), he was making $160 a month. Another year and another railroad later (the Chicago Great Western), he reached $200. After two years there, he was promoted to superintendent of motive power at $350 a month — the top mechanical job in railroading.

His next step appeared to be in reverse — back into overalls at $275 a month for American Locomotive Company in the manufacturing end of railroading. But within two years, he was works manager at $8,000 a year. He had been raised to $12,000 when General Motors offered him half that amount to become works manager of Buick in 1911. He took the job and the $6,000 cut in pay — and moved his wife and four children to Flint, Michigan to begin one of the most remarkable careers that can be found in an industry that is filled with remarkable careers.

In 1914, Walter Chrysler was making $25,000 a year. The next year, he was general manager of Buick at $50,000. In 1916, he had a clear choice of becoming a partner in a rival automobile company — or remaining as the new president of Buick at $500,000 a year. After some hesitation, he decided to stay with Buick.

From a salary of $6,000 to $500,000 in five years is a fairly good jump in pay — especially when the income tax on it was almost nothing. It becomes even more remarkable when we learn that Chrysler's total yearly income was actually in the vicinity of a million dollars a year because he chose to accept almost all of his pay in the form of General Motors stock. Let's see if it is possible to discover why someone thought he was worth that kind of money.

When Walter Chrysler started with Buick, the company was producing about 45 cars daily. Within six months, and with essentially the same men and equipment, he had increased production to 75 cars a day. He quickly followed Henry Ford's lead in installing a moving assembly line for more efficient production. And he adapted to automobile production the excellent cost accounting system he had learned at American Locomotive. For the first time in the history of the company, it then became possible to figure in advance the exact cost of producing a Buick.

In 1915, Buick production exceeded 44,000 cars. One year later, it reached 125,000. Meanwhile, Chrysler was drawing on his long experience as a master of machines and a manager of men to improve the quality of the Buick automobile while steadily decreasing the cost of producing it. And also meanwhile, the value of General Motors stock (of which Buick was the keystone) was steadily rising. While many persons were responsible for the success of General Motors during those years, no one questions the fact that Walter Chrysler was primarily responsible for Buick's magnificent production and profit record. Rather than lose his vast knowledge of machines, methods, and men (especially to a competitor), the officials of General Motors made him that fabulous offer. Perhaps he would have stayed for less, but it is by no means certain.

Over the next three years, both General Motors and Buick continued to expand — with Buick accounting for almost half of G-M's total profits during that period. In 1919, Walter P. Chrysler, president of Buick and vice president of General Motors in charge of operations, found himself in almost complete disagreement with the policies of his boss, the equally dynamic William C. Durant. So, even though he was offered still more money to stay on, Chrysler decided to retire — age 45, a multi-millionaire.

As could easily have been predicted, the retirement was strictly temporary. Mr. Chrysler often joked that he actually did intend to retire, but that his wife didn't like him hanging around the house all day. So after a few months of boredom, he let it be known that he was again in the market for another job. He soon got one — in fact, two at the same time.

The 1920-21 depression was a disastrous time for automobile companies. When it hit, almost all of them were in an overextended and vulnerable position. During that period, more than half of them failed, were reorganized, or were absorbed by other companies. As we already know, Walter Chrysler's former employer, General Motors, was in serious trouble along with the rest. But the two companies that here concern us are Willys-Overland and Maxwell-Chalmers.

A group of banks held $50 million in notes of the Willys-Overland Company, and $26 million in notes of the Maxwell Motor Company. Since both of those long-time producers of automobiles were faced with immediate bankruptcy, the noteholders organized themselves into management committees to save whatever they could from the debacle. None of them knew much about the business of operating an automobile company. So it is hardly surprising that they turned to a man who did — Walter Chrysler.

First, he was asked to act as the bankers' representative in the management of Willys-Overland. A year later (and with the agreement of Willys), he undertook the reorganization of Maxwell at the same time. His conditions for accepting the two jobs were similar: First, he was to be in full charge. Second, for a period of two years, Willys-Overland was to pay him a salary of one million dollars a year, net. And Maxwell was to pay him $100,000 a year, plus an option on a large block of stock. The bankers and the companies quickly accepted his terms.

In both companies, in turn, Chrysler followed much the same procedure. He began by making various needed changes in management. A few officials lost their jobs, many others had to accept a heavy cut in salary, and there was a general shifting around of responsibilities. He sold a number of both companies' less productive properties, and consolidated others. He also disposed of large amounts of surplus inventory. He persuaded various manufacturers and suppliers to cancel the too-heavy commitments for parts and materials that had been placed with them by both companies. He even negotiated more favorable terms for both Willys-Overland and Maxwell from the very bankers who had hired him to save their money! In due course, he brought in a few new men and began the necessary research for a better car. And, although his primary job was "managerial fireman" (especially at Willys-Overland), he automatically gave much thought and time to the problems of how to improve production and sales.

When his two years were up at Willys-Overland, the banks had been paid back more than half of their loans. The remainder of that debt was retired by a bond issue, and the company was put through receivership and reorganized under new management. By then, Walter Chrysler was devoting his full energies to Maxwell. Perhaps a subconscious reason that had caused him to accept stock, instead of more money from Maxwell, was that he had been smitten by that wonderful but rugged American dream of "going into business for yourself."

Soon after he had accepted the Willys-Overland job offer, Walter Chrysler had commissioned a team of consulting engineers — Fred Zeder, Owen Skelton and Carl Breer — to design a better engine for a new car for that company. They did, but Durant Motors eventually bought it for the Flint car. When Chrysler became top man at Maxwell-Chalmers, he hired those three engineers as a team to become a part of that organization. Under the leadership of Fred Zeder, Chrysler himself worked along with the others in building a new engine for a Maxwell car. When the engine was finished, they were so impressed with its performance that they decided to design a completely new

1928

PLYMOUTH

1959

1928

DE SOTO

1959

133

1925

CHRYSLER

1959

car around it. The startlingly new "Chrysler" was unveiled in the lobby of the Hotel Commodore in New York City in January of 1924. It was an instantaneous success.

The next year, Maxwell Motor Corporation went through a friendly reorganization and the Chrysler Corporation was born. At that point, the new company was thirty-second down the line among producers of automobiles. The new president and chief stockholder of Chrysler Corporation set out to improve that position. He began by hiring a few more selected men with the various talents that a large company must necessarily have. Chief among them was K. T. Keller, a fellow-mechanic he remembered from his days with General Motors.

Mr. Keller had begun his career as an apprentice mechanic in the Westinghouse machine shop. At age 24, he was assistant to the superintendent of the Westinghouse automobile engine department. Later, he was a foreman for the Metzger Motor Car Company. At age 27, he became the master mechanic of Buick. His boss there was Walter Chrysler. Mr. Keller was general manager of the Canadian Division of General Motors when Mr. Chrysler offered him the job of general manager of Chrysler Corporation in 1926. He took the job — and eventually succeeded Walter Chrysler as president in 1935. (The third and current of the three Chrysler presidents is L. L. Colbert, 1950, whose legal work for the corporation had so impressed both Chrysler and Keller that they hired him as general counsel for the company in 1933.)

With his team of engineering, production, marketing, and legal specialists — plus the financial genius of B. E. Hutchinson whom he had hired as treasurer in 1921 — Walter Chrysler was soon challenging the top leadership of the automobile industry. In addition to launching two new cars in 1928 — Plymouth and De Soto — the Chrysler Corporation also bought out and absorbed the Dodge Brothers automobile company. In less than a decade, Chrysler Corporation rose from its thirty-second spot to the number two position behind General Motors in the production of automobiles. And, along the way, Walter Chrysler became an exceedingly wealthy man.

Most of us can appreciate the logic of a high salary and other benefits to the person who builds a small business into an industrial giant. Such a man becomes everybody's favorite; even his competitors generally admire and respect him. The stockholders naturally think he's wonderful because he makes them a lot of money. The employees like him because their jobs become the most desirable and most secure in the industry. The customers obviously prefer him to his competitors because he gives them a better product at a better price. To the public in general, he often becomes a kind of folk hero. Since the story of his drive to the top is usually a dramatic one, his name is constantly in the newspapers and magazines. In some respects, such a man often enjoys the popularity that is usually reserved for a top movie star or sports figure. His high pay isn't begrudged because everybody has a pretty good idea of what he has done for it. Walter Chrysler held such a position in general public esteem. So did Henry Ford and a score or more other pioneers among those early automobile men.

But when the company is firmly established and the "second and third generation" management takes over — well, that's different. The drama is usually gone. People imagine that the hard part has already been accomplished, and that now it's only a simple matter to keep the company going. It is generally assumed that it should be easy enough to find any number of men capable of doing that — and at a comparatively modest salary. But as is only too well illustrated by the decline and fall of 25 or so companies that were once giants in the automobile business, such men are exceedingly rare.

Actually, the management that could have *prevented* the decline and failure of any one of those companies would have been just as valuable to the owners and employees and customers as was the management that built it into a profitable enterprise in the first place. That's why it is almost impossible to overpay the management of a large corporation that shows a constant growth and profit over the years. But for some strange and most unfortunate reason, the fact that superior management is a rare quality isn't understood at all by the general public. For if we did understand it, we would also understand why they are worth exceptionally high salaries.

Chapter 10
WHERE MEN ARE FREE TO TRY

Over the past two centuries, millions of men have used countless billions of words in an effort to describe the essence of the idea that is summed up in the word "America." We have national, state, and local contests for pupils who write essays on "What America Means To Me." We have an "I Am An American Day" at which top speakers try to capture the spirit behind those words. Sermons and books are devoted to the theme. It is a favorite subject for newspaper editorials throughout the year. But no one has ever yet told the story to the satisfaction of all concerned. No one ever will. It's too big, and it means different things to different people. But certainly one of the many ideals that are typical of America is that men shall be free to choose the careers they wish to follow, and that they shall stand or fall on the wisdom of their own choices and the results of their own efforts. Perhaps the following brief story of the parallel careers of two men will serve to illustrate one aspect of that ideal in practice.

Elliot J. Russell (of whom you never heard) and Frederick J. Fisher (the eldest of those seven famous "Body by Fisher" brothers) were those two men. And as we shall see, they had considerably more in common than a middle initial. They were fairly close to the same age. The grandfathers of both had migrated from Europe to the United States in search of a better opportunity for their skills and talents. Both boys completed "grammar school" in their respective states of Virginia and Ohio. Both then became skilled craftsmen in trades based on horse-drawn transportation; Russell was a top-notch harness maker, and Fisher was an equally expert carriage maker. Both left home at the turn of the century to seek their fortunes elsewhere — the one to Manning, South Carolina, the other to Detroit, Michigan. Both of those skilled craftsmen quickly found jobs — the one in a combination livery stable and harness shop, the other in a company that made bodies for both horse-drawn vehicles and those new-fangled horseless carriages. And in due course, their respective employers made both of them superintendents over many men. But neither was satisfied to stop there; each wanted to go into business for himself. And since they lived in a country where a man controls his own fate, they both did it.

Within a month of each other in the summer of 1908, two more small businesses were started on their uncertain ways toward success or failure. One was named the Russell Harness Shop in Burlington, North Carolina; the other was known as the Fisher Body Company in Detroit, Michigan. The first one involved a total capital of perhaps around $5,000 — and the proprietor was the sole owner. The other one had a paid-in capital of $30,000 — supplied by Fred J. Fisher, his partner and younger brother Charles T., and their uncle Albert. Both of those small businesses were successful from the start. The Russell Harness Shop soon expanded into bigger quarters, and the work force was increased from one to four. The Fisher Body Company also soon needed more space and more employees.

As you are doubtless well aware, the similarity of those parallel stories ends at this point. But the fact that one of those men became exceedingly wealthy, while the other one didn't, is merely incidental to this story. The point of interest here is that both men were free to try. Both did try.

Before we continue the story, let's pause a moment and imagine that some newspaper in 1908 had conducted a "public opinion survey" concerning the probable success of those two men. Both were in their thirties when they established their businesses. Both were skilled and ambitious artisans who were tops in their trades, and both possessed a native intelligence that was surely well above average. While no two men are ever equal in these respects, let's assume that the people being interviewed would have been unable at that point to observe any particular difference in their degrees of skill, ambition, and intelligence.

The key survey question would probably have been something like this: "One of these young men has stated that the automobile will never displace the horse, and thus he is casting his lot with the animal that has served man since the dawn of history. The other is of the opinion that the automobile is far more than a passing fad and a plaything of the rich, and thus he is risking his money and his future on that new form of transportation. Which do you think will be the more successful?"

There is almost no doubt that the horse-conscious people of that day would have voted overwhelmingly for the cautious and realistic maker of saddles and harness. After all, 52 of those new automobile companies had failed in the depression of the previous year! So the young man who would deliberately choose to base his future on such an uncertain business as building bodies for automobiles, must be foolish indeed. And he shouldn't blame anyone but himself for what would probably happen to him.

Fortunately, the decision to try or not to try was left to the judgments of the two individuals concerned, instead of to the majority of the people. There was no law and no tradition to prevent either of those men from following his own ideas as he saw fit. Each of them had an equal chance to realize the full potentialities of his skills and wisdom. It was strictly the personal choice of each man as to how he would use his time, talents, and money. *That* is the traditional American concept of equality of opportunity. Under that concept, what one does with his opportunities (if anything), isn't too important; that's his problem, and he should be eternally grateful it is. Even the level from which he starts isn't at all vital; while it's certainly nice to be fortunate enough to begin with a superior education and a large amount of capital, that is totally unrelated to equality of opportunity. And fortunately for most of us, it isn't necessary for ultimate success. The only really vital issue is that no law shall prevent the ambitious person from trying. That's the essence of equality of opportunity, and it's worth fighting for.

The end of the story of the harness maker is quickly told. For many years, he earned an excellent living for his family. In due course, he was making the harness for most of the horses in his community. And his reputation as an artist in leather became so widespread that his finely-tooled saddles for show horses found a ready market well beyond his own community. Then one day, he lost his biggest account — the fire department of Burlington. switched from horses to trucks. That was a vast improvement for everybody concerned — except, perhaps, the harness maker and his employees. He had to let one man go. Then another. Finally there were no employees. He was back where he had started. One of his grandsons recently summed it up rather neatly when he quipped, "Grandpa bet on the wrong horse."

Thousands of those "horse oriented" small businessmen all over the nation were suffering the same fate. Almost none of them failed in the traditional sense; they just sort of slowly declined and withered away with the horse. But hundreds of similar small businessmen were astute enough to realize what was happening. They understood that the horse age was drawing to a close, and that the future belonged to the automobile. So they converted from making equipment for horses to making equipment for automobiles. Unquestionably, the most successful among them were Fred J. Fisher and his brothers.

When the Fisher Body Company was formed, there were more than 100 firms in the Detroit-Flint area making bodies for both automobiles and horse-drawn vehicles. One was the largest automobile body maker in the world — the C. R. Wilson Company for which both of the elder Fisher brothers had worked. One of the reasons that quickly established Detroit as a center for automobile production was the availability of so many carriage makers in the area; both the required skill and the needed wood products were immediately available to supply the bodies for those early automobiles that were mostly conventional buggies without the customary horse.

The Fisher tradition of fine workmanship in body building started with the grandfather in Germany. His son carried on the

1959 American Motors Rambler 4 door

1959 American Motors Rambler Station Wagon

1959 American Motors 2 door American

1959 American Motors Metropolitan

143

Studebaker-Packard Corp. 1959 4 door Lark

Studebaker-Packard Corp. 1959 2 door Lark

Studebaker-Packard Corp. 1959 Lark Station Wagon

tradition in Norwalk, Ohio. In turn, most of the grandsons learned the same trade by working in that small family business. So it was only natural that they should have given due consideration to the possibility of building bodies for the carriage without the horse. From the beginning, they were thinking in terms of *closed* bodies for automobiles. And during their first two years as a company, they experimented with a few single orders for individual persons who wanted closed bodies built on the automobiles they had already bought. It was not until 1910, however, that they got their first big order — 150 closed bodies for Cadillac.

Soon thereafter, they took a lead in the body building business that they never lost. In 1916, their plant had a capacity of around 400,000 bodies a year — still mostly open bodies, of course. At that time, their corporation was valued at about $4 million. Three years later, it was worth around $45 million.

Then William Durant's expansion program for General Motors reached out for the Fisher Body Corporation — with mixed results. Most of the Fisher Body products were already being sold to G-M, but by no means all of them. In turn, General Motors bought most of its bodies from Fisher, but it also had other sources of supply. Even so, the mutual dependence was such that both were naturally concerned about the future relationship between them. For obvious reasons, neither wished to become completely dependent on a single customer or a single source of supply. Apparently, G-M was the more worried of the two. But when Durant first offered to buy Fisher Body, he received a flat refusal. It seems that for two or so years previous to that time, the Fisher brothers had been considering the possibility of making cars as well as bodies. If such a venture were successful, obviously they would no longer have to worry about a customer for their bodies! But they finally decided against it. Thus when Durant of G-M called again, they were in a mood to listen. In 1919, General Motors bought three-fifths of Fisher Body for $27.6 million, with the understanding that the Fishers were to continue to manage it. In 1926, G-M purchased the other two-fifths through an exchange of stock.

If the Fishers had decided to build their own car, the history of the automobile business might well have been considerably different from what it is today. But at best, that is pointless speculation. Beginning in 1919, the Fishers cast their lot with General Motors. By 1927, three of the brothers were on the G-M Board of Directors. In due course, a fourth one also became a director. It is often written and said by responsible people in Detroit that General Motors as we know it today is certainly as much — and possibly more — the handiwork of the Fishers as of any other comparable group.

"Body by Fisher" was already a valuable sales point for an automobile before General Motors bought control of the company. After that, it became even more so. That famous emblem that identifies a Fisher body was derived from the designs of two of the world's most famous coaches — Napoleon's coronation coach and the one he used for his marriage to Marie Louise. The Fishers wanted that emblem to represent both quality and style. From the day they made their first car body, they devoted their fabulous energies and skills to the building of a body that wouldn't rattle and squeak after a few miles of use over the rough roads of that time. They were eminently successful.

After joining General Motors, the Fisher Body Division of that company continued to contribute to the advancement of comfort and safety in automobile bodies. Its No Draft Ventilation system of the early 1930's was particularly notable. But, next to the perfecting of the closed body itself, the greatest advance in automobile body building was the discovery of a practical way to paint them in the early 1920's. That development was not due to the efforts of Fisher Body as such. It was a joint General Motors-du Pont project. But since automobile bodies were concerned, naturally the Fishers were in it from the beginning.

Henry Ford once said that "any customer can have a Ford

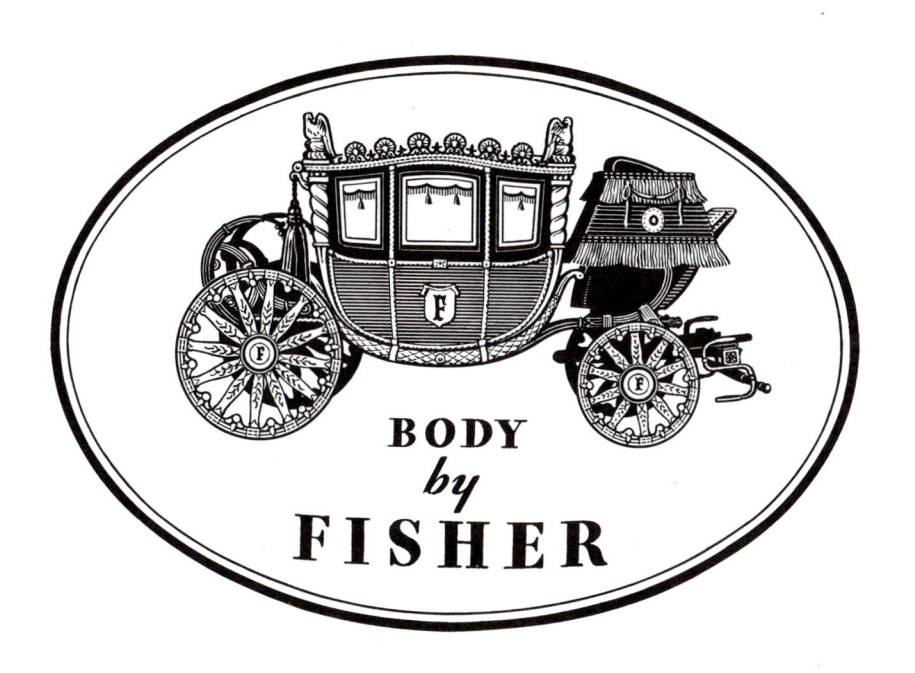

First closed Body by Fisher, 1910

THEN . . .

AND NOW

car painted any color he wants, so long as it is black." At the time, most people probably interpreted his remark as merely another one of those famous Model T jokes. Perhaps a few might have thought of it as an unfortunate example of arrogance. The remark, however, was actually prompted by an entirely different reason. In the early 1920's, the time required to paint a car in color varied from 15 days for the cheaper models up to 30 days for the more expensive ones. There just wasn't enough covered storage space in all Detroit and Flint to hold the number of cars that rolled off those assembly lines in a period of 20 days or so. Thus, literally, they couldn't be painted in colors. One automobile manufacturer humorously suggested that the needed drying space for such a job would require that a roof be built over the entire state of Michigan. At any rate, the cost of building the needed storage space — plus the cost of painting the cars and holding them off the market for three weeks while they were drying — would certainly have added 50 to 100 dollars to the sales price. But as long as the finish was the customary black enamel, the job of painting and heat-drying a car body could be completed in an hour or so. Thus Ford's classic statement was based on the economics of the situation, not on humor or arrogance. If the cost could have been held down, those Model T's would have appeared in every color of the rainbow. (In fact, as any Ford man will proudly inform you, quite a few of those Model T's were both enclosed *and* colored.)

General Motors was, of course, having the same trouble. While many of its Fisher bodies did appear in color, the added cost was naturally passed along to the purchaser. But since it was obvious that the customers wanted their cars in color, G-M appointed a "Paint and Enamel Committee" under the direction of its Research Director, Charles Kettering, to see what could be done.

That 1921 committee first consulted the paint and varnish manufacturers. The committee asked them to produce a paint that would dry in less than 17 hours instead of the customary 17 days. The paint must also be as inexpensive as the current enamel process. In addition, it must be available in all colors, and last as long as the automobile body itself. Those paint manufacturers said it couldn't be done.

General Motors' paint committee soon discovered that toy manufacturers were already using a cheap, colored, and fast drying lacquer with a cellulose nitrate base. The only trouble with the lacquer was that it dried *too* fast. In fact, it dried before it could even be sprayed on the car! That lacquer, however, did supply a clue to the solution. Cellulose nitrate or "gun cotton" is the base of smokeless powder. So the G-M paint committee decided to consult the chemists of du Pont, the nation's largest producer of smokeless powder. Strangely enough, they discovered that those chemists were already working on the problem for another reason. So the scientists of General Motors and du Pont joined forces, with those of du Pont playing by far the leading role in the search. In 1923, they found what they were looking for — a lacquer finish that could be manufactured cheaply in any color, could be applied and dried in seven hours, and was even more durable than enamel. (They soon discovered that it also served equally as well as an attractive finish for furniture, radios, refrigerators, and other similar equipment.)

The 1924 Oakland line of cars was the first to appear with the new colored finishes. They were a sensation. The next year, all General Motors cars were available in various colors at no increase in price. While the cheapest of those G-M "Body by Fisher" cars still cost $100 or so more than Henry Ford's Model T, the customers began switching by the hundreds-of-thousands from black and open Fords to colored and closed Chevrolets. Certainly those closed and colored bodies by Fisher were a primary reason for General Motors rapid surge into first place ahead of Ford in the mid-1920's.

When people are free to try, it's impossible to predict either the results or the winners. But one thing *can* be predicted: We consumers will thereby have the best possible chance of getting whatever it is we most want. More progress and prosperity for more people will come from that type of economy than from any other. Another vivid example of how it works can be found today in the no-holds-barred competitive struggle that is being waged by American Motors Corporation to persuade you to buy its small or compact car instead of a big car. (The same thing, of course, also holds true for Studebaker-Packard with its Lark.)

American Motors came into existence on May 1, 1954, through a merger of Nash-Kelvinator and Hudson Motor Car Company. Shortly thereafter, the various banks that held millions of dollars in notes on that company would gladly have sold them for less than 50 cents on the dollar. For it seemed almost certain that American Motors was soon to suffer the same sad fate as all the previous producers of small cars in the United States — starting with the one and two passenger Cyclecars of 1913 and continuing over the years with the Whippet, Austin, Willys, Bantam, and others. But American Motors did not fail — for the simple and conclusive reason that we consumers began buying Ramblers.

Why we began buying them is of no importance to this study. Whatever our reasons, our purchases increased in 1956. The trend continued steadily upward in 1957 and 1958. While "big three" sales were declining, Rambler sales shot up to a new high. According to three important measurements that were available in the last week of 1958 — sales, plant expansion, and stock market prices — it appears that the "big three" could easily become the "big four." And according to those same tests, Studebaker-Packard also shows signs of climbing back to the heights once held by its ancestors.

There is absolutely nothing to prevent American Motors from displacing General Motors as the top producer of automobiles — if it can supply us consumers with a product we want at a price we are willing to pay. Contrary to all the erroneous reasoning you may have heard about "monopoly" in the automobile industry, consumer approval is still the determining factor for success. Without it, no company (regardless of size or resources) can continue to stay in business. No company has ever had a monopoly in the automobile industry. In no sense does a monopoly exist today. Nor can a monopoly ever exist in an economy that permits you and me to compete — along with Willys Motors, Checker Motors, International Harvester, General Electric, Mad Man Muntz, the Aluminum Company of America, Westinghouse, Volkswagen, and any other organization that might think it profitable to begin producing automobiles. All of those above organizations — plus more than 10,000 others — either have produced cars, are now producing them, or would be most happy to enter the automobile business if they believed they could improve upon either the price or the quality of the cars now being offered to us. We need a law to protect us against General Motors just about as much as we need a governmental decree to ban the common cold.

It is completely pointless to argue that companies should be of a certain size, or that we should or should not have small cars, or cars with or without chrome. For as long as men are free to try, you will soon be offered any type car you want. And, as usual, the manufacturer who offers us what we want (at a price we are willing to pay) will become both wealthy and big. The manufacturer who tries to sell us a car we don't want — or tries to charge us more than we are willing to pay for it — will go bankrupt.

That's the heart of our competitive economy and its resulting high level of living. For purely selfish reasons, we consumers decide which automobile manufacturer shall fail and which shall succeed — and that's the way it should be.

Chapter 11
THE SILENT PARTNER

As we noted in the first paragraph of this brief study of the automobile, Oliver Evans was granted a patent for a self-propelled road carriage during the same year that the founders of this nation drafted the Constitution of the United States. In the preceding chapters, a summary of the development of the automobile — and its widespread impact on the way we live — has been given. This concluding chapter is dedicated to the role played by a "silent partner" — government — in the development of the automotive industry as we know it.

We Americans are only 6.4 per cent of the world's population, living on less than six per cent of the world's land area. But we produce more than 60 per cent of the world's cars, trucks, buses, tractors, and other such automotive equipment. We also lead every other nation in the production and use of steel, rubber, oil, clothing, books, housing, medicines, meat, milk, and almost any other product or service that the people want or need. The reason for our productive leadership is *not* natural resources; for several other nations equal or excel us in that respect. Nor are we inherently more intelligent than others; for, after all, we Americans are merely a conglomeration of peoples from every nation on the face of the globe. And certainly we don't work any harder than the people of various other countries. Thus the only major difference between us and others would appear to be our form of government. For a moment, let's return to that Constitutional Convention of 1787 and try to discover just what those founding fathers were trying to accomplish.

The primary objective of our forefathers was to insure maximum freedom of action and equality of opportunity to every citizen in his personal and business affairs. To insure that primary objective of the Revolution, the founders of this nation designed a cumbersome governmental system of checks and balances, of limited powers, and much division of those powers between the federal and state governments. And by arranging for frequent elections of officials, they hoped thereby to prevent any one person or group from holding for long the few powers that the government did have. With a few minor exceptions, the founders did all in their power to bar the government from the general area of economic activities. In fact, they deliberately designed one of the most *economically inefficient* forms of government ever known. The reason for that becomes more understandable when we remember that they had just led a successful rebellion against the planned economy of the government of King George III. They were in no mood to endorse in a new form what they had just rejected in an old form.

Except in time of war, the government wasn't expected to do much of anything. And it didn't. It bumbled along slowly and inefficiently, generally doing only those few things that had to be done in order to keep it operating at all. On occasions, the duly elected and appointed officials of our government rose to great heights of statesmanship. On other occasions, they sank to equally great depths of sordid log-rolling. All in all, the system of government established by our forefathers was a pretty good mechanism to insure the primary objective for which it was established — maximum freedom for the individual citizen.

In the area of economic goods and services, the government generally confined itself to encouraging and aiding others (both persons and companies) to exploit, develop, and settle the nation. Throughout the early history of our nation, the main highways were generally built and operated by private turnpike companies. Water transportation was controlled by private interests. The railroads were all privately owned. The active part played by government varied from nothing to very little in meeting the economic needs and desires of the people. Never before in the history of the world had a government sat idly by while its people did almost anything they wanted to do. And as a direct result of that inactivity, this nation experienced a release of human energy and accomplishment that astounded the world.

Were there injustices? Of course there were. Was there suffering? Yes, there was. Did some persons exploit other persons? They did. Were the votes and influence of some senators and governors for sale? They were — and they were bought. Was there any favoritism? There was indeed. Were there many examples of greed, stupidity, and outright criminality? Yes, there were countless such examples — by both governmental and private interests.

Point out all the mistakes and evils you wish (they are easy enough to find), and then look again at the overall record. Never before in all history were so many people so well fed, clothed, and housed. There was more laughter and human happiness in this land than in any other. Never before had the world ever witnessed such an outpouring of the material things of life — as well as an unparalleled abundance of charity, love, and respect for the individual person. Thousands and hundreds of-thousands of schools and churches sprang up across the land. Here the Biblical injunction to feed the hungry and clothe the naked became a part of our daily lives. Provision was made for the widow and the orphan, the sick and the poor, the halt and the blind. We first helped ourselves, and then we helped our less productive neighbors — both at home and abroad. For the most part, our government remained strictly passive in the market place. It seldom concerned itself with what was produced or how it was distributed. And millions of people from lands where governments actively participated in both production and distribution, came pouring into the United States.

They came in search of opportunity for themselves and their children. Here a man could work for others or for himself. Here there was no state religion, no heredity nobility, no rigid class barriers, and, especially, no governmental controls over economic affairs. Here a man was his own master, and both he and his children could rise as high as they were capable of rising. Many of them became rich and famous, and almost all of them improved their lot in one way or another. There were no price controls, and food and manufactured products were both plentiful and cheap. There were no wage controls, and wages were the highest in the world. There were no limits to the profits a man could make, but he had to produce something the people wanted to buy before he could make any profit at all. We were the "melting pot" — for dreams and economic ideas, as well as for persons with different backgrounds. We were a brawling, sprawling melange of all races, religions, nationalities, and languages. Among us were the ambitious and the lazy, the weak and the strong, the fool and the genius, evil men and honorable men. We could (and did) tolerate strange religious ideas. We could (and also did) tolerate equally foolish ideas about carriages that would run without horses.

Meanwhile, the government continued its traditional policy of doing mostly nothing — except to act as a sort of referee that did a reasonably fair job of restraining murderers, robbers, and outright frauds. The government didn't concern itself at all about Oliver Evans and his ideas for a road vehicle that would run under its own power. True enough, the new government granted him a patent, but what he did with it was strictly up to him. When Charles Goodyear patented his method for vulcanizing rubber in 1844, the government obviously knew about it since a patent was involved. But it showed no further interest in the process. (The commissioner who issued that patent, Henry Ellsworth, stated in his 1844 Annual Report that "The advancement of the arts from year to year taxes our credulity and seems to presage the arrival of that period when human improvement must end.")

As far as can be determined, the government knew nothing at all about the world's first oil well that was brought in by E. L. Drake at Titusville, Pennsylvania in 1859. The govern-

a. b. c. d. e. f.

a. The first wheel. A section of log.
b. Babylonian chariot wheel. 4000 B.C. Wood held with copper clamps.
c. Egyptian chariot wheel. 1500 B.C. Wood with rawhide tires.
d. Roman chariot wheel. 300 A.D. Wood, highly decorated.
e. American Covered Wagon wheel. 1750. Wood with iron tire.
f. American automobile wheel. 1906. Wooden spokes with pneumatic tire.

Photo Courtesy Goodyear Rubber Co.

RUBBER

Photo Courtesy American Petroleum Institute

OIL

ment had neither encouraged nor discouraged him. The problem of what to do with the oil (if anything) was left strictly with "Colonel" Drake. In due course, the government also issued patents on several types of internal combustion engines that had been invented or improved upon by its free citizens — but that's all it did. And when John B. Dunlop, a Scottish veterinary surgeon living in Belfast, Ireland, first developed his idea for an air-filled rubber tire, neither London nor Washington knew anything about it. Dr. Dunlop was merely trying to devise some way to prevent his young son from shaking himself to pieces as he rode his iron-tired bicycle over the cobblestoned streets of that city. When his idea proved to be a practical success, both his government and ours learned about it only when he applied for a dual patent in 1889. While bicycle companies in both countries were most interested in his invention, neither of the two governments appeared to care about it one way or the other.

When, in 1893, the Duryea brothers used a by-product of Colonel Drake's oil to supply the power for their "horseless carriage," our government had no idea at all that America's first practical automobile was finally in operation. The officials in Washington couldn't have cared less.

Nor did the government have any interest at all in the first factories built specifically to manufacture automobiles in 1899 — the Olds gasoline cars in Detroit, Michigan and the Stanley Steamers in Tarrytown, New York and Bridgeport, Connecticut. The government treated R. E. Olds and those twin brothers (F. O. and F. E. Stanley) exactly as it was later to treat Henry Ford and the thousands of other persons who went into the automobile business — it just ignored them entirely. When, over the years, almost all of those automobile companies failed and went out of business, the government did nothing. When a few of them succeeded and made fortunes for the owners, the government continued to do nothing.

Nor did the government in any way encourage Captain

Anthony F. Lucas as he began drilling into those strange "dome formations" he had observed all along the coasts of Louisiana and Texas. Actually, Captain Lucas was mostly interested in finding salt and sulphur. He was about as astounded as anyone else on January 10, 1901 when his drilling rig was hurled skyward by the fantastic gusher of oil he had tapped at "Spindletop" near Beaumont, Texas. There was a good market for sulphur and salt, but about the only use for oil lay in the kerosene that could be refined from it. One cynic looked at that 160 foot geyser of gas and oil and asked Lucas, "What are you going to do with it — feed it to the longhorns?" Captain Lucas found the answer to his problem in Detroit, *not* in Washington. In due course, the booming automobile industry began using so much gasoline — the "useless" by-product of oil — that millions of persons all over the world were soon depending on it for their livelihoods. Until the oil industry was a highly successful business, the government left it completely alone.

In short, it is safe to say that the government played no part whatever in the development of the automobile and the primary industries based on it — except the crucially vital part of doing absolutely nothing, one way or the other. And for that, we are forever indebted to the founders of our nation who deliberately planned it that way.

True enough, the government did build almost all of the roads the automobile now runs on. But it is doubtful if anyone will claim that our highways have kept pace with the development and needs of the automobile. Even if the proposed Interstate Highway System is completed, the overall road situation will still be grossly inadequate for the amount and type of traffic it must carry.

A student of this problem once succinctly summed up the difference between public and private development of transportation facilities in this novel manner: Suppose, he said, that around 1900, the government had decided to assume full responsibility for developing and building automobiles — and had left the building of roads to private enterprise. What might have happened? He predicted that, under those circumstances, we would today have a highway system far superior to the few, crude automobiles that would have been produced by government. (And he might well have added that a privately-owned "General Roads Corporation" would probably be running a national contest to solicit ideas whereby government might be encouraged to build more and better cars to run on the private highway system.) Actually, of course, we can never know what might have been. But we do know beyond any shadow of a doubt that the government's roads have not kept pace with the development of the automobile.

In no sense is this a criticism of government as such. Actually, when all is said and done, our government has done a far better job of road building than we had any reason to expect. And as time goes on, perhaps it will do an even better job. Even so, we are fortunate indeed that the developing and building of our automobiles, railroads, and airplanes was left mostly to private initiative. We are further fortunate that the actual building of our highways is also done by private construction companies, with the government confining itself to a supervisory capacity. Otherwise, the present deplorable situation might well become intolerable.

Be that as it may, the traditional American role of government as a "silent partner" has been steadily changing over the past 50 years or so in all economic areas. It is changing because we citizens want our government to become more active in our daily affairs. In no sense is the change due to any "plot," either foreign or domestic. We ourselves demanded it and voted for the persons who promised to do it. And as was to be expected, we are getting what we want.

Perhaps we are wise enough (and are now experienced enough) to keep our active and largely unrestricted government within reasonable bounds. Perhaps we aren't. No one can say with absolute certainty. But this much is sure: The continuing trend toward more active participation by our government in our daily affairs and problems is a complete reversal of the principles laid down by the founding fathers in 1787.

Today, it is becoming increasingly popular to scoff at their concepts of eternal principles, personal responsibility, and severely limited governmental powers. Those ideas of our forefathers are now often called "horse and buggy" principles that might work in a frontier community but not in an industrial age of rapid transportation and communication. The fact remains, however, that it was those "horse and buggy" principles themselves that caused the development of the automobile and the countless other products and services that have made this earth a more pleasant place to live. Conversely, the world-wide situation that has been threatening for so many years to plunge us back into the barbarism of complete governmental controls is due almost exclusively to a rejection of those principles and concepts — in *all* nations, including our own.

The conviction that success will come to "the man who builds a better mousetrap" is traditional among American businessmen — including, of course, those persons who invent and manufacture the thousands of parts and accessories that make up a finished automobile. The story of the Atwood Vacuum Machine Company is offered here as an example of that theory in practice.

In 1909, two young brothers — J. T. and S. B. Atwood — established a small company in Rockford, Illinois to manufacture those newfangled vacuum cleaners that enabled the housewife to do a better cleaning job with less effort. While the new venture was successful, it could hardly be called spectacular. After several years in business, the two brothers themselves were still a noticeable percentage of the work force.

Then, in 1916, came the idea for the better mousetrap. Seth B. Atwood became the proud owner of a new Maxwell — but the doors rattled something awful. Instead of merely complaining to the manufacturer, however, "S. B." invented a "door bumper" that stopped the rattling. In due course, almost all of the automobile companies were installing those "door silencers" on their new cars. During the middle 1920's, the Atwood Vacuum Machine Company reached a yearly output of 21 million of those adjustable steel stampings with rubber inserts for doors.

Today, the company manufactures a complete line of "body hardware" — hood, door, and trunk hinges; seat adjusters; door latches, trunk and hood locks, brake mechanisms, and other assemblies: With 1,800 employees — and five plants in Canada and the United States — it is a highly successful manufacturer of automobile parts and other equipment.

Throughout its 50 years of operation, the Atwood Vacuum Machine Company has remained a family enterprise. In 1953, Seth B. Atwood moved up to chairman of the board, but still remains as active and forceful as ever. His son, Seth G., succeeded him as president. And if one of the young sons of the new president should develop both the desire and the ability to follow the family tradition, doubtless he also will have ample opportunity to try his hand at running the business at some future time. That possibility — freedom to build for one's children and for one's children's children — is unquestionably the mainspring of America's greatness. Without it, the dream that has been America would be finished.

The author is pleased to dedicate this Special Edition of "Men, Motors, and Markets" to the Golden Anniversary of the Atwood Vacuum Machine Company and the ideal it represents.

Seth B. Atwood, Chairman of the Board, receives a golden trowel from the contractor as the cornerstone for a new plant is laid. At his left is his brother James T. Atwood, Chairman Emeritus, and at his far right is his son Seth G. Atwood, President.

Bibliography

Allen, F. L. *The Big Change*. N. Y., 1952.
Anderson, Rudolph. *The Story of the American Automobile*. Washington, 1950.
Automobile Manufacturers Association, Detroit: *A Chronicle of the Automobile Industry in America, 1893-1953. Automobile Facts and Figures* (Annual). *Motor Truck Facts* (Annual).
Bathe, Granville, and Dorothy. *Oliver Evans*. Philadelphia, 1935.
Beasley, Norman. *Knudsen: A Biography*. N. Y., 1947.
Borth, Christy. *Masters of Mass Production*. N. Y., 1945.
Burlingame, Roger. *Backgrounds of Power*. N. Y., 1949.
Chrysler, Walter, and Boyden Sparkes. *The Life of an American Workman*. N. Y., 1950.
Cleveland, R. M., and S. J. Williamson. *The Road is Yours*. N. Y., 1951.
Cohn, David. *Combustion on Wheels*. Boston, 1944.
Denison, Merrill. *The Power to Go*. N. Y., 1956.
Doolittle, J. R. *The Romance of the Automobile Industry*. N. Y., 1916.
Epstein, Ralph. *The Automobile Industry*. N. Y., 1928.
Ford, Henry, and Samuel Crowther. *My Life and Work*. Garden City, 1922.
Ford, Henry, and Samuel Crowther. *Today and Tomorrow*. Garden City, 1926.
Garrett, Garet. *The Wild Wheel*. N. Y., 1952.
Glasscock, C. B. *The Gasoline Age*. N. Y., 1937.
Holbrook, Stewart. *The Age of the Moguls*. Garden City, 1953.
Kennedy, E. D. *The Automobile Industry*. N. Y., 1941.
Kouwenhoven, John. *Made in America*. Garden City, 1948.
Lewis, Eugene. *Motor Memories*. Detroit, 1947.
Lynd, Robert, and Helen. *Middletown*. N. Y., 1929.

MacManus, Theodore, and Norman Beasley. *Men, Money and Motors.* N. Y., 1929.
Merz, Charles. *And Then Came Ford.* Garden City, 1929.
Morris, Lloyd. *Post Script to Yesterday.* N. Y., 1947.
Musselman, M. M. *Get A Horse!* N. Y., 1950.
Nevins, Allan, and Frank Hill. *Ford: The Times, The Man, The Company.* N. Y., 1954.
Nevins, Allan, and Frank Hill. *Ford: Expansion and Challenge.* N. Y., 1957.
Partridge, Bellamy. *Fill 'er Up!* N. Y., 1952.
Pound, Arthur. *The Turning Wheel.* Garden City, 1934.
Richards, William. *The Last Billionaire; Henry Ford.* N. Y., 1948.
Seltzer, Lawrence. *A Financial History of the American Automobile Industry.* Boston, 1928.
Sinsabaugh, C. G. *Who, Me?* Detroit, 1940.
Sloan, Alfred P., Jr., and Boyden Sparkes. *Adventures of a White-Collar Man.* N. Y., 1941.
Stark, George. *City of Destiny.* Detroit, 1943.
U. S. Committee on the Judiciary (Senate). *A Study of the Antitrust Laws.* Washington, 1956.
U. S. Federal Trade Commission. *Report on Motor Vehicle Industry.* Washington, 1939.

Plus various releases and booklets from the American Automobile Association, the Automotive Safety Foundation, the Chrysler Corporation, the General Motors Corporation, the Ford Motor Company, and others.

Index

A

Accident rates, 82, 92, 93, 95, 98
Action Program of the President's Committee for Traffic Safety, 96
Advertisements, 28n
Agriculture and automobiles, 71, 75, 82
American Locomotive Company, 129
American Motors Corporation, 117, 151
Americanism, 113, 139, 153, 163
Anderson, Robert, 12
Armament production, 38, 44, 47, 50
Atwood, J. T. and S. B., 1, 163
Atwood Vacuum Machine Co., 1, 163
Automobile industry
  agriculture affected by, 71, 75, 82
  Atwood Vacuum Machine Co., 1, 163
  competition and, 110, 149
  development of, 3
  education affected by, 63, 78, 90, 95
  electric power of, 18
  executives in, 101, 113, 127
  Fisher Body Company of, 139, 145
  free enterprise and, 113, 139, 153, 163
  German, 13, 21, 113
  government and. See Government
  improvement in, 33, 37
  increased use of, 21, 33, 55, 82
  insurance companies and, 98
  investments, 101, 114, 118
  monopoly and, 151
  parts manufacturers, 1, 163
  production. See Production
  races, 21, 28n
  small, 151
  taxation and, 63, 89
  vacation travel and, 58
  wages, 56, 106, 127
  war effects on, 38, 44, 47, 50
  women and, 31, 34, 67
  see also, name of automobile or company under subject
Automobile Manufacturers Association, 92
Automotive Council for War Production, 47, 48
Automotive Safety Foundation, 90, 92, 96

B

Benz, Karl, 13
Billionaires, 101
Blanchard, Thomas, 7
Brayton, George, 13
Breer, Carl, 132
Bryan, Jimmy, 32
Buick Motor Company, 115, 129, 130
Burke, Alice, 34
Burlingame, Roger, 10

C

C. R. Wilson Company, 142
Cadillac, 22, 145

167

Capitalism
 American, 113, 139, 153, 163
 industrial, 9
 production under, 41, 153
 Russian view of, 42
 slavery affected by, 8, 11
Chevrolet Motor Company, 117
Christianity and slavery, 9
Chrysler, Walter P., 128
Chrysler Corporation, 135
Communism and production, 41, 53
Competition, automotive, 110, 149
Constitutional Convention, 3, 153
Consumption. See Production
Cotton gin and slavery, 11
Cowles, E. P., 85
Cugnot, Nicholas, 4
Cuneo, John Newton, 31
Curtice, Harlow H., 120

D

Daimler, Gottlieb, 13
Daimler Motor Company, 113
Death rate, 82, 92, 93, 95, 98
Depression, 41, 131
Detroit automotive industry, 44, 139
Dewar, Thomas, 22
Dodge Brothers, 135
Donner, Frederic G., 120
Dort, Josiah Dallas, 115
Drake, E. L., 156
Driver education, 63, 78, 90, 95
Dunlop, John B., 14, 159
du Pont, Pierre A., 118
Durant, William C., 115, 117, 130, 145

Durant-Dort Carriage Co., 117
Durant Motors, 132
Duryea, Frank and Charles, 14, 25, 113

E

E. I. du Pont de Nemours Co., 117, 150
Education
 effects on, 63, 78, 90, 95
 safety, 97
 slavery and, 8
Edwards, Gus, 26
Eisenhower, Dwight D., 44
Electric power, 18
Elgin Road Race, 28n
Ellsworth, Henry, 156
Employment
 executive, 101, 113, 127
 Ford, 112
 slave, 8, 11
 women, 67
England
 automobile club in, 22
 slavery in, 10
 steam engine in, 4, 12
Evans, Oliver, 3, 153
Executives, automotive, 101, 113, 127
Eystron, George, 33

F

Farming. See Agriculture
Federal Highway Act of 1956, 85
Fisher, Frederick J., 139
Fisher Body Company, 139, 145
Flint Road Cart Company, 117
Food production, 75
Ford, Edsel, 124

Ford, Henry
  investments of, 114
  painted cars of, 146
  race cars and, 26
  success of, 101, 105
Ford, Henry II, 124
Ford Foundation, 112
Ford Motor Company, 101, 114, 119, 124
France
  automotive industry in, 13, 39, 113
  steam engine in, 4
Free enterprise. See Capitalism

G
Gasoline engine, 13, 18, 113
General Motors Corporation
  Chrysler, Walter P. in, 129
  executives of, 115
  Fisher Body Company and, 139, 145
  highways and safety program of, 85
  Paint and Enamel Committee of, 149
Germany
  automotive industry in, 13, 113
  race cars in, 21
Glidden, Charles J., 28, 31
Glidden Tours, 28
Goodyear, Charles, 156
Gordon, John, 120
Government
  automotive industry and, 153, 160
  farmers affected by, 75
  highways, 85, 89, 160
  noninterference of, 156
  safety education and, 97
  slavery and, 8

Graham, Hannah, 34
Gurney, Goldsworthy, 7

H
Hancock, Walter, 7
Hanks, Sam, 32
Harroun, Ray, 32
Highways
  government, 85, 89, 160
  politicians and, 96
  safety and, 85
  transportation on, 56
Hoover Research Committee on Social Trends, 69
Hutchinson, B. E., 135
Hyatt, Roller Bearing Company, 119

I
Income
  automotive, 56, 106
  executive, 101, 113, 127
  investments and, 101, 114, 118
Indianapolis Speedway, 32
Industry
  automobile. See Automobile industry
  oil, 156, 160
Insurance, automobile, 98
Internal combustion engine, 38, 159
Interstate Highway System, 86, 160
Investments, automotive, 101, 114, 118

J
John R. Keim Mills, 119

K
Kahn, Albert, 112
Keim Mills, 119
Keller, K. T., 135

Kettering, Charles, 34, 149
Khrushchev, Nikita, 43
Knudsen, William S., 44, 119

L

Labor. See Employment
Lenoir, Jean Joseph Etienne, 13
Levassor, Emile, 17
Louisiana Purchase Centennial, 28
Lucas, Anthony F., 160

M

Macauley, Alvin, 47
Malcomson, Alexander, 103
Management, automotive, 101, 113, 127
Marx, Karl, 8
Maxwell-Chalmers, 131
Maxwell Motors Company, 131
McCormick, Cyrus Hall, 76
Medical care, 82
Memorial Day Sweepstakes, 32
Metzger Motor Car Company, 135
Model T, 106
Monopoly, automotive, 151
Moses, Robert, 85
Murdock, William, 7

N

Nash, Charles W., 116
Nash-Kelvinator and Hudson Motor Car Co., 151
Nash Motor Company, 117
Nation, Carrie, 34
Neustadt-Perry Company, 26
Newcomen, Thomas, 4

O

Oil industry, 156, 160
Oldfield, Barney, 27
Olds, R. E., 159

Orukter Amphibolos, 3
Otto, Nikolaus, 13

P

Paint and Enamel Committee of G-M, 149
Panhard-Levassor, 113
Parts manufacturers, 1, 163
Patens, 13, 37, 112, 156, 159
Politicians and highway safety, 96
Power, source of, 17
Production
   agricultural, 71, 75
   armament, 38, 44, 47, 50
   Detroit, 44, 139
   free enterprise and, 41, 113, 139, 153, 163
   mass, 25, 101, 110, 150
   Russian, 41, 53
   taxation and, 63, 89
   war, 38, 44, 47, 50
Profits, automotive, 101, 114, 118
Public works, highway, 85, 89, 160

R

Races, automobile, 21, 28n
Richardson, Nell, 34
Roberts, Montague, 21
Robertson, George H., 34
Rochas, Beau de, 13
Roper, Sylvester Hayward, 22
Royal Automobile Club of London, 22
Russell, Elliot, J., 139
Russell Harness Shop, 140
Russia, production in, 41, 53

S

Safety and highways, 85, 96

Salaries, executive, 101, 113, 127
Schuster, George, 21
Selden, George, 14
Selden patents, 37, 112
Sir Thomas Dewar trophy, 22
Skelton, Owen, 132
Slavery, 8, 11
Sloan, Alfred, Jr., 119
Songs about automobiles, 26
Speculation, 101, 114, 118
Sports car races, 21, 28n
Standard Highway Safety Program for States, 96
Standard of living
  American, 41, 81, 112, 114, 153
  Russian, 41
  slavery and, 8, 11
Steam engine, 3, 12, 17
Stephenson, George, 7
Stock car races, 21, 28n
Stockholders, automotive, 101, 114, 118
Strelow, Albert, 101

T

Taxation, 63, 89
Thomas B. Jeffery Company, 117
Thomas Motor Car Company, 22
Transportation
  agriculture and, 71, 75, 82
  effects on, 3, 56
  public vs. private, 160
  safety, 85
Travel, automotive, 58

U

United Motors Corporation, 119

V

Vacation industry, 58
Vanderbilt, William K., 28
Vanderbilt Cup, 27, 34
Verne, Jules, 21

W

Wages. See Income
War
  automobile industry and, 38, 44, 47, 50
  economic effects of, 42
Watt, James, 4
Wells, H. G., 9
Westinghouse, 135
White, Walter C., 33
Whitney, Eli, 11
Willys-Overland Company, 131
Wilson, Charles E., 119
Winton, Alexander, 25, 27
Women and automobiles, 31, 34, 67

Z

Zeder, Fred, 132

171